We all Want to Change the World

The Life of John Lennon

We all Want
to Change the World

The Life of John Lennon

John Wyse Jackson

Originally published in
Great Britain in 2005 by
Haus Publishing Limited
26 Cadogan Court
London SW3 3BX

A CIP catalogue record for this book
is available from the British Library

ISBN 1-904950-37-X

Designed in Adobe InDesign CS2
and typeset in Plantin by Rick Fawcett

Printed and bound by Graphicom, Vicenza, Italy

www.hauspublishing.co.uk

Contents

I am not in the group of people who think that because all our dreams didn't come true in the Sixties everything we said or did was invalid. No, there isn't any peace in the world despite our efforts, but I still believe the hippie peace-and-love thing was worthwhile. If somebody stands up and smiles and then gets smacked in the face, that doesn't invalidate the smile. It existed.[1]

– John Lennon.

There, there's a place, Where I can go, When I feel low, When I feel blue, And it's my mind, And there's no time, When I'm alone.

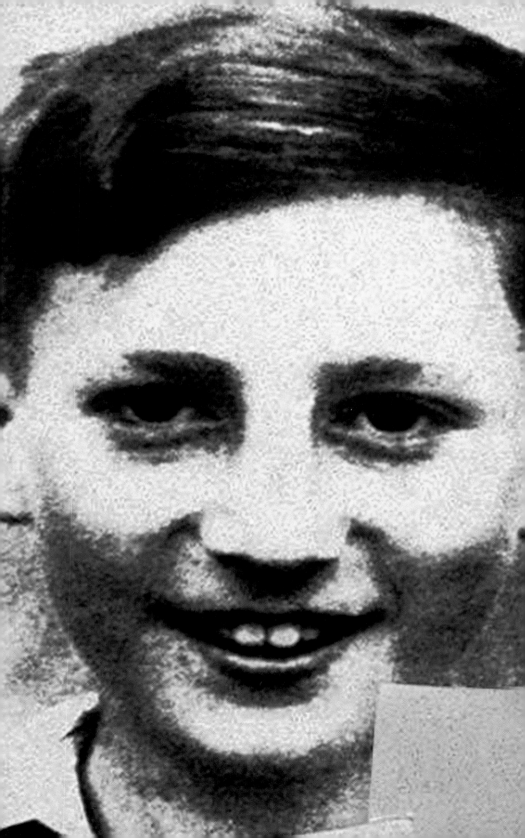

Sitting in an English Garden[3]

'Liverpool is where the Irish came when they ran out of potatoes,'[4] John Lennon once put it. There were so many Irish in Liverpool that in England it used to be called, he said, 'the capital of Ireland.'[5] Each of the Beatles had Irish blood flowing through his veins, but of the four none had more than John Lennon. It was a lineage he was proud of. In 1970, he told an interviewer: 'I heard country-and-western music in Liverpool before I heard rock 'n' roll. The people there – the Irish in Ireland are the same – they take their music very seriously.'[6] John Lennon took his music very seriously too. He called it art.

On his father's side all John's known forebears were accomplished musicians. His earliest identified Lennon ancestor was his great-grandfather, also called John Lennon, who was born in Dublin during the first half of the 19th century. Family lore remembers him as a ship's cook who had sung for pennies with his father in alehouses along the west coast of Ireland. Neither calling can have been very successful, for around the mid-century, soon after the Great Famine, he left Ireland with his wife, Elizabeth (née Morris), and their two sons, Jack and William.

Just where the family settled at this stage is unclear. They probably came to Liverpool. William became a Catholic priest in St Joseph's Church, Blundellsands, Liverpool, but

11

in 1905 was put on permanent sick leave after some obscurely scandalous episode, most likely involving mental problems or drink – though the family preferred to hint of an affair with a housekeeper. His brother Jack enjoyed greater success as a popular singer and soloist with 'Andrew Roberton's coloured operatic Kentucky Minstrels', and toured with them (in blackface) in the United States during the 1890s. Jack Lennon must have returned to Ireland at least once: after appearances there in 1897 Roberton's troupe was described by the *Limerick Chronicle* as 'the world's acknowledged Monarchs of refined Minstrelry,' while the *Irish Times* said that they were 'undoubtedly the finest organisation of Minstrels that ever appeared in Dublin.'[7]

After he married, Jack gave up performing and settled down in Liverpool, where he found work as a shipping clerk. As his American wife had died while giving birth to a daughter, he hired a Liverpudlian woman, Mary ('Polly') Maguire, to look after the child. Polly was illiterate, but she had Irish roots, and it was a fruitful alliance. They may never have married, but they were happy together, and over the next few years she presented Jack with eight more children. The first two were baptised as Roman Catholics like their father, but after both died in infancy Polly insisted that the others be brought up in the Church of England. One of these, the couple's fourth surviving son, was Alfred ('Freddie') Lennon, John's father.

Freddie Lennon was born in 1912. His childhood was somewhat Dickensian. At first he lived with the family at 27 Copperfield Street, Toxteth, a tiny house in a terrace near the Liverpool docks. In later life he remembered sitting on his father's knee as he performed minstrel songs and routines from his glory days on the stage. Jack Lennon was a keen gambler: as soon as his ship came in, he used to promise his wife, he would have them all 'farting against silk'.[8] In the Irish way, verbal dexterity was much admired among the Lennons, and one of Freddie's main legacies from his father would be his ability to turn a pithy phrase, a talent that in turn John Lennon would inherit. Jack's public appearances

12

were now confined to the local pubs, so money was always in short supply, and when he died in 1921, Polly was unable to support her large family alone. Freddie, now aged eight, and his sister Edith were sent to be fed and educated in the city's Bluecoat orphanage school, in the Penny Lane area, though they still saw their family during holidays. Bad nutrition had already left the boy half crippled with rickets, then a common affliction among the children of the urban poor, and though he was forced into shameful iron braces, his legs would always remain stunted. As an adult Freddie was sensitive about his height, five feet four inches. (One day his famous son would say 'He looks like a little one of me, only he's five foot tall.')[9]

Despite this affliction, Freddie was an enthusiastic showman like his father, and he was a good singer. From an early age he also had a talent for slapstick, and could play the harmonica. At the age of 14 he ran away from the orphanage and after an audition was invited to join a stage show of juvenile entertainers run by Will Murray, a comedian and theatrical manager who had once worked with Charlie Chaplin and Stan Laurel. Freddie accompanied them to Glasgow, pursued by an orphanage official, and was dragged back and mocked in front of the whole school for imagining that anyone whose legs were so short could ever be successful on stage. A year later, out of the orphanage for good, he was taken on as a bellboy on the *SS Montrose*, a Cunard liner cruising the Mediterranean. Freddie Lennon had found his vocation.

He met John's mother in a Liverpool park the same week he left the orphanage. Born in 1914, Julia Stanley was then an attractive, mischievous girl of fifteen, the fourth and most flirtatious of the five daughters of 'Pop' Stanley, an official with a deep-sea salvage company. They became friends at once. Over the next years, as Freddie Lennon worked his way up to senior steward on the great transatlantic cruise liners of the 1930s, he experienced the happiest period of his life, running ship's concerts and dreaming of his girl in Liverpool. On stage, he performed Al Jolson's songs, singing in blackface like his father, and he appeared with a false toothbrush moustache for his celebrated impersonation of Adolf Hitler. He once even conducted an orchestra in Lisbon. As his son John would conclude: 'I think Fred must have been popular. He used to send us ship's concert lists with his name on, singing "Begin the Beguine".'[10]

Every time Freddie returned from his trips, he used to appear on George Stanley's doorstep and invite Julia out. They would meet up with some of his brothers and play music together – she was learning to play the banjo. After some ten years of this, on 3 December 1938, they suddenly got married, apparently 'just for a joke'. Their honeymoon was a visit to the Forum Cinema, which aptly was showing *Dr Barnardo's Homes* with Mickey Rooney. Afterwards, her marriage still unconsummated, Julia went home alone to her parents' house to break the news. 'You'll have more dinner times than dinners,'[11] said her mother, who had always disapproved of 'that Alf Lennon'.[12] Freddie had disappeared off again to the West Indies within the week.

The couple's first and only child was conceived during one of Freddie's fleeting visits to Liverpool, and was born on 9 October 1940. It was the year after the outbreak of World War II, while the city and its important docklands were suffering the close attentions of Hitler's Luftwaffe. A myth has spread that the evening of the birth was portentously marked by the worst bombing raid of the war, but despite the insistence of some of the family, records show that the skies were clear that night. The baby was christened John Winston Lennon. His middle name, chosen by Julia, was a tribute to the Prime Minister, then struggling to keep Britain and the world free for democracy, but his first name was in honour of his Lennon grandfather, Jack, the man who had made Freddie into an entertainer.

Julia's eldest sister Mary (whom everyone called Mimi – all the Stanley girls had nicknames) was a former nurse. She was the most capable, and the bossiest, of the sisters. Her husband, George Smith, dairy owner and failed amateur bookie, was a gentle soul, kept firmly under the control of his formidable wife. Mimi had decreed that the couple

14

Julia Lennon and the infant Victoria, John's 'lost sister', in 1945

would never have children: having looked after her younger sisters while they were growing up, she had already had quite enough of that sort of thing. But when Mimi saw her new nephew, she fell in love with him. 'I knew the moment I saw John in that hospital that I was the one to be his mother and not Julia,' she once told an interviewer. 'Julia accepted it as something perfectly natural. She used to say, "You're his real mother. All I did was give birth."'[13] Before long she had persuaded Julia to move into a nearby cottage that George had inherited, where she would also be close to yet another sister, Harriet ('Harrie').

Away from her father for the first time, Julia was soon spending her evenings in the pub. Sometimes she used the doting Mimi or Harrie as babysitters; sometimes John was simply left on his own. One night, it seems, he 'saw a ghost just outside the window and screamed with terror until the neighbours came round to investigate.'[14] With Freddie off at sea, Julia started various love affairs. An interlude with a Welsh soldier led to a daughter, patriotically named Victoria Elizabeth, who was born on 19 June 1945. Pop Stanley and Mimi together bullied Julia into giving the baby up for adoption. John knew nothing of his lost sister until 1964, when he asked his aunt Harrie about his memory of 'a very grey side to Mummy. I remember often going into her bedroom and seeing her crying. She seemed very sad at times.'[15] Aunt Harrie then decided to tell him the probable reason.

But for Julia, life had to go on, and within a short time, ignoring the existence of her lovelorn seafaring husband, she had moved to a one-room flat with a man she had met from the catering trade, called John ('Bobby') Dykins. Mimi promptly appeared on the doorstep with a social worker in tow, pointing out that the accommodation was shockingly unsuitable for a child: her beloved nephew was sleeping in the same bed as the couple, who were not even married to each other. When she offered to take John off her mother's hands, Julia gave in without a fight. Before John Lennon was six, he was living with Mimi, George, and several cats at 251 Menlove Avenue, a busy main road going through the former village of Woolton, to the south-east of Liverpool.

'There were five women that were my family,' John Lennon would later recall. 'Five strong, intelligent, beautiful women, five sisters. One happened to be my mother. My mother just couldn't deal with life. She was the youngest. And she had a husband who ran away to sea and the war was on and she couldn't cope with me and I ended up living with her eldest sister.

'Now those women were fantastic. One day I might do a kind of Forsyte Saga just about them. I always had it in the back of my mind, because they were fantastic women and they dominated the situation in all the family. The men were just invisible in our family. I was always with the women. I always heard them talk about the men and talk

16

about life, and they always knew what was going on. The men never, never ever knew.'[16]

In contrast to his mother's flat in grimy Gateacre in the Penny Lane area of the city, John's new home was 'a nice semi-detached place with a small garden and doctors and lawyers, and all that, all living around.'[17] A man from Uncle George's dairy came in twice a week to do the garden, where John would play and have picnics with his cousins when they came round. The 1930s villa, which had a panelled hall complete with grandfather clock, even boasted a name, 'Mendips'. He had his own bedroom with a view. Mimi later spoke of her very early days with John: 'I used to send him off to bed, panda under one arm, teddy under the other. And he sang himself to sleep every night. We so enjoyed having him, they were the best years of my life bringing him up.'[18] The two men of the house, Uncle George and John, quickly became very close, even conspiratorial. As a necessary refuge from Mimi's sharp tongue, they went on expeditions in the countryside around Woolton and shared little secrets together. A good amateur artist, Uncle George encouraged his nephew to draw and paint, and every night would read him a bedtime story, to be rewarded at tucking-up time with 'squeakers'[19] (John's word for kisses).

Over the next ten years Mimi worked hard on her nephew, trying to treat him like a son by dispensing discipline and love (albeit undemonstrative love) in equal measure, passing on her values and giving some structure to his life. She too even tried to foster his artistic talents, in her way: 'I used to do embroidery,' John would proudly recall in 1980. 'My auntie told me how to do little flowers.'[20] He was taken to the cinema twice a year without fail, given bicycles in due time and, it is said, a pony. But for John, initially at least, the nightmares were never very far away, as Mimi remembered: 'On the bus going to town he wouldn't sit with me. He'd go to sit at the top, and I'd sit at the door, in case he'd run out, you know. He'd be looking down at me and say, "You haven't forgotten me, have you?" "No, I haven't," I'd say. He was lovely.'[21]

17

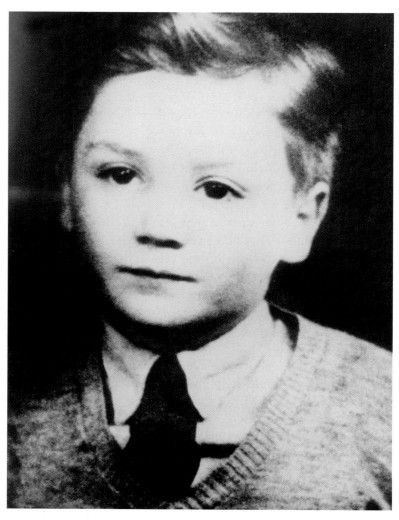

John Winston Lennon, in his primary school uniform

Whatever Mimi Smith's deepest motives for wishing to bring up her sister's child, as a nurse she was convinced that her charming, feckless sister had been in danger of damaging John for ever. The signs were plain to see. When still only five, before she had rescued him, John had already been expelled from his first school for infants, Mosspits Lane, for bullying a girl. The main problem was that he loved his real father, Freddie, whom he hardly ever saw, while he regarded the substitute one his mother was offering him, Bobby Dykins, with jealous loathing. Mimi believed that the sooner John forgot about his early life the better. 'I never told John about his father and mother,' she informed the biographer, Hunter Davies. 'I just wanted to protect him from all that. Perhaps I was overanxious. I don't know. I just wanted him to be happy.'[22] Though John would never fail to express his gratitude for what his Aunt Mimi had done for him, the relationship between them was not always easy, and too many secrets were being kept. More than twenty years would have passed, and John would be famous as the leader of the most successful pop group in history, before he discovered that nobody had been telling him the whole story about his early years, or the real reason why his father had disappeared, apparently without a word . . .

The truth was that Freddie had not deserted his son, as both Mimi and his mother would always claim. Though he was often away for long periods (like many other Liverpool sailors), he always hoped that the family would stay together. Before Victoria was born, he even offered to accept the baby as his own if it would help matters, but Julia turned him down. A little later, Mimi phoned him and said that John had appeared on the doorstep, having run away from Julia and Dykins, who were neglecting him. Freddie came as soon as he could and, much to John's delight, Mimi let him take his son out for a walk. But, instead of bringing him back again, Freddie whisked John away to Blackpool, where he had friends they could stay with. Father and son had a lovely holiday together there – and there is a family memory that John was even taken to Dublin for a few days by one of his uncles. Freddie pondered his options, which seemed to come down to two: either to emigrate with John to New Zealand, or to have him adopted by Freddie's brother Sydney and his wife Madge. But, not untypically, two months had passed before any decision was reached.

On 22 June 1946, Freddie and John were tracked down by Julia, who appeared on the doorstep with Dykins. Freddie pleaded with her to come to New Zealand too, but she refused.

Then she addressed John directly: which of his parents did he want to stay with? Twice, John chose his father. But then, after Julia had turned on her heel and left, John shouted 'Come on, Daddy,'[23] and ran after her down the street. Freddie knew that if he loved his son he would have to let him go. The battle was over. Back in Liverpool, Julia quickly sent John back again to live with Mimi and George. The next time Freddie got in touch, Mimi told him to stay away from John, and refused to pass on messages. For John, the whole disturbing episode would become like a confusing dream. 'I soon forgot my father,' he later commented.[24]

At his new school, Dovedale Primary, the headmaster paid John something of a double-edged compliment, telling Mimi, 'There's no need to worry about him. He's as sharp as a needle. But he won't do anything he doesn't want to.'[25] Though John seems to have been a reasonably good pupil at first, after he had made his first few friends the rot rapidly set in. 'I'd been honest at Dovedale, if nothing else, always owning up,' he claimed later. 'But I began to realize that I was foolish.'[26] Ivan Vaughan, a classmate whose garden adjoined Mimi's, introduced him to another neighbour, Nigel Walley, and to Pete Shotton, a ragamuffin with a shock of fair hair and a devilish grin. Before long John was their leader.

Over the next few years, the boys roamed free around the nearby lanes and fields, crossing on homemade rafts to treasure islands in Jackson's pond, playing football in the cow field on the top of Woolton Hill, kicking the tops of green Liverpool buses from overhanging trees on Menlove Avenue, dodging nuns in the woods around the Strawberry Fields Orphanage, trying to derail trams, shoplifting in Penny Lane, terrorizing girls and generally getting into trouble. Once, John was shot at for stealing apples. On the evening before Guy Fawkes night one year, John and Pete lit the enormous annual Woolton bonfire: local fury was so great that there was certainly no question of owning up to that.

'I had a feeling that God might have visited St. Peter's, the local church, but that he actually preferred it outdoors. I certainly did.' The first money John Lennon ever earned

20

from music was as a member of the choir there, which paid a very worthwhile two shillings and sixpence per wedding. He went with his friends to the Sunday School Bible Class too, not only because attendance was rewarded with annual seaside outings on the train to Southport, but also because it gave him a public arena for participating in lively debate (or showing off). When at one session he caused a commotion in the Church Hall by hotly arguing that the Scribes and Pharisees who denounced Jesus must have been Fascists, he was caned with a crocodile-handled umbrella by the Rev Maurice Pryce Jones, the 'Welsh vicar who hated children . . . I can see him now with his well-fed Christian face, his high-pitched voice and his mouth in a permanent wave, a Sunday smile.'[27] John Lennon and Pete Shotton were the only ones ever to be kicked permanently out of both Sunday School and the Choir. To everyone's despair, the two boys were becoming virtually unmanageable when they were together, which was a great deal of the time.

Pete Shotton was the first of John's 'other halves', or partners in life, a series which would go on to include Paul McCartney, Stuart Sutcliffe (the 'lost Beatle') and Yoko Ono. 'In my company', Pete would recall later, '[John's] humour was often deadpan in the extreme; he could make me laugh with just a word, a subtle inflection in his voice, or an almost imperceptible gesture . . . You might say that he would transmit to me by stages his own mental picture of a situation. As I tuned into his vision, my laughter would inspire him to elaborate further . . . "Let's hear you squeak, then, Pete," John would say, deliberately winding me up yet more, until I'd not only writhe helplessly on the floor, but would actually develop excruciating stomach cramps and a temporary blindness brought on by uncontrollable tears of laughter.'[28] 'Shennon and Lotton,'[29] as John called them, would never desert each other.

Mendips was a bookish household, with a library 'full of Oscar Wilde and Whistler and Fitzgerald and all the Book of the Month Club stuff that my auntie had around.'[39] Uncle

21

*John's bedroom and the sitting room in Mendips, now restored
and preserved by the National Trust*

George had taught John to read by the time he was six, getting him to puzzle out headlines in the local paper. John's favourite comic was the *Beano*; but he also soon developed the habit of reading books, and loved how they allowed him to travel to strange new worlds in his mind. It was a habit he would never lose, and his first creative impulses would tend towards writing rather than music. When he was still only seven, he published (in an edition of one) *Sport, Speed and Illustrated*, an anthology of his own verses and stories, adorned with cut-outs of film and soccer stars. One birthday he was given *Alice in Wonderland* and *Through the Looking Glass*: he read them again and again, and composed new versions of the verses embedded in the text. Lewis Carroll, and particularly his poem about the grotesque monster, the Jabberwock, full of 'portmanteau' words, would lie behind much of John's later prose. Carroll would also colour such songs as 'Lucy In The Sky With Diamonds' and (more explicitly) 'I Am The Walrus'. He went on to read and love Kenneth Grahame's *The Wind in the Willows* and Stevenson's *Treasure Island*.

Richmal Crompton's books about William Brown and his gang of four, the Outlaws, would become particular favourites. John wrote his own versions of the William stories too, starring himself, and it is easy to see why the young John Lennon should have been attracted to this untidy, rebellious, plain-speaking schoolboy. The *Just William* stories are set in a genteel English suburb not unlike Woolton. William scorns all adults and their obsessions, such as dressing smartly, and working, and girlfriends. He only wants to be left alone to pursue his schemes with the Outlaws, and perhaps to raise a little money for sweets. When these perfectly reasonable objectives are vetoed, William usually achieves them anyway, by cunning. If in the process he accidentally catches a crook or saves a cottage from burning down, so be it, but he has never sought the gratitude of adults, because William DOESN'T CARE.

With Nigel Walley, Ivan Vaughan and Pete Shotton, John now had his own gang of 'Outlaws'. The friendship between Lennon and Shotton in particular was deplored by both

Aunt Mimi and Pete's mother, Bessie, each woman blaming the other's boy for being a 'bad influence'. At least the two were at different schools: otherwise neither would have had a hope of passing his 11 plus examination, and would never have made it to Quarry Bank Grammar School.

As it was, John got through his exam in style and in September 1952 joined Quarry Bank. So did Pete Shotton. One of the 'better' secondary schools in Liverpool, it was, like the great Etonian public schools upon which it was modelled, an old-style single-sex establishment featuring masters in gowns, pupils divided into 'houses,' and the cane. For lessons, the boys were streamed according to their ability: thanks to their good exam results, both John and Pete were put into the 'A' stream. Aunt Mimi had high hopes for John.

So it was that there began a running battle with the school authorities that would last for five years. Every morning John and Pete cycled off together in the direction of school, but they did not always get there. When they did, they were disruptive, rude, lazy and dishonest. For John, one problem was that his teachers did not recognize just who it was they had sitting in front of them: 'When I was about 12, I used to think I must be a genius but nobody'd noticed. I thought, "I'm a genius or mad. Which is it? I can't be mad because nobody's put me away – therefore I'm a genius."'[31]

The young Lennon offered his teachers very little evidence of his genius, unfortunately. Apart from constant witticisms and hurtful remarks, the only manifestation of anything unusual was to be found in a confiscated exercise book that made them laugh in the staff room. This was *The Daily Howl*, a parody newspaper that John produced irregularly, mostly for Pete Shotton's benefit. It was made up of stories, drawings and mock news reports, often concerning maimings or death: 'Our late editor is dead, he died of death, which killed him. His wife married again the day he died, and sold his possessions which he owned. She said she was sure that it was the way he would have wanted it.' With its puns – 'Peace on earth and good wool to all men' – and its double takes – 'Today has been dry, except for

24

the wet periods (which were wet)'[32] – *The Daily Howl* drew on Spike Milligan's *Goon Show*, John's favourite BBC radio programme, though it was driven by his interest in death and crippledom, subjects which would be hallmarks of John's writing for years to come. His obsession with cripples may have begun one day on a drunken walk with Pete in their early teens, as he would recall: 'Liverpool is full of deformed people, the way you have them in Glasgow, three-foot high men selling newspapers. I'd never really noticed them before, but all the way home that day they seemed to be everywhere. It got funnier and funnier and we couldn't stop laughing.'[33]

Invariably accompanied by Pete, each school year John was demoted, first to the 'B' stream and then to the 'C', where he took up residence close to the bottom of the class. Every term, in report after report, Aunt Mimi had to read verdicts like 'Attitude in class most unsatisfactory,' or 'Poor. He never makes any really sensible effort.'[34] Late in John's school career Mimi took him for an eye test, and discovered that he had never been able to see the blackboard properly. She bought him a pair of heavy black-rimmed spectacles, as he refused to wear the round ones issued free by the National Health. But by then, it was far too late. The constant lines, detentions and beatings continued, and at least once John was suspended from the school for a week. Beneath the crest on his black blazer was the school's motto in Latin, which read *Ex Hoc Metallo Virtutem* – Excellence Out Of This Base Metal. As far as most of his teachers were concerned, excellence seemed an impossible objective for John Lennon: indeed, he appeared to be getting baser by the week.

Every summer, between the ages of nine and 15, John was packed off by Mimi for a fortnight or so to the north-western tip of Scotland, where at Durness her sister Elizabeth ('Mater'), the wife of an Edinburgh dentist, had a family croft surrounded by wild mountains, moorland and bogs. Mater's son Stan, seven years older than John and rather a hero of his, was always there, and sometimes other cousins. Even though they still occasionally called John 'Stinker', a nickname had earned as a toddler, he treasured these times with his extended family, and developed an unlikely love of salmon fishing. He would keep in affectionate (if erratic) touch with them all his life. The spectacular, primal landscapes of the highlands fed directly into John's growing sense that he was important, that he must be an artist. 'I was kind of hallucinating. The ground starts going beneath you and the heather, and I could see this mountain in the distance. And this kind of feeling came over me: I thought, "This is something! What is this? Ah, this is that one they're always talking about, the one that makes you paint or write because it's so overwhelming that you have to tell somebody . . . so you put it into poetry."'[35]

In June 1953, when John got home from perhaps the last of these holidays, Mimi told him that his Uncle George had died suddenly of a haemorrhage while he was away. He was only 52. John later recalled his reaction: 'I didn't know how to be sad publicly – what you said or did – so I went upstairs. Then my cousin [Leila, Aunt Harrie's daughter] arrived and she came upstairs as well. We both had hysterics. We just laughed and laughed. I felt very guilty afterwards.'[36]

George Smith had given John the first musical instrument that he ever learned to play reasonably well, a cheap harmonica. At idle moments he could now take his 'mouthy' from a back pocket and play 'Greensleeves' or 'The Happy Wanderer'. John had been very fond of his uncle, but his friends might not even have been told about his death. He never spoke very much about his life at home, and indeed rarely brought anyone back to face Mimi. However, there was one member of his family he would soon be happy to share with the rest of his gang, an amazing woman about whom he really knew very little. Julia Lennon had just come back into his world.

In fact John had never entirely lost sight of his mother, who had occasionally appeared at the house to talk to Mimi about problems she was having with Bobby Dykins. She once upset him by arriving at 'Mendips' with blood streaming down her face, but no explanation was ever offered. 'My feeling never died off for her. I often thought about her, though I never realized that she was living no more than five or ten miles away. Mimi never told me. She said she was a long, long way away.'[37] Actually Julia's house was barely three miles away in Allerton, where she lived with Dykins and their two daughters, Julia and Jacqui. After George's death, when John finally found out where his mother was living, from time to time he would bunk off school and cycle to her house, sometimes with a friend in tow. Pete Shotton remembers the first time he met her: he was 'greeted with squeals of girlish laughter by a slim, attractive woman dancing through the doorway with a pair of old woollen knickers wrapped around her head . . . Rather than shake my proffered hand, Julia began stroking my hips. "Ooh, what lovely slim hips you have," she giggled.'[38] Heady stuff for 13-year-olds.

When Aunt Mimi felt that she was being treated badly by John, she could be formidable. Once, after he had stormed off to stay at Julia's after a row, she reduced him to tears by having his beloved dog put down – he was now obviously far too busy with his mother to be bothered bringing poor Sally for walks any more. Mimi disapproved of her sister's devil-may-care attitude to life, and was jealous of John's relationship with her. Now that George was gone, she missed even more the lively loving little boy that John had once been. Mimi's feelings at this time, and perhaps also her words, are echoed in lines that John would one day insert into a song of Paul's ('She's Leaving Home'): 'We gave her most of our lives . . . Sacrificed most of our lives . . . We gave her everything money could buy . . . We never thought of ourselves . . . Never a thought for ourselves . . . We struggled hard all our lives to get by . . . What did we do that was wrong . . . We didn't know it was wrong.' The song concludes: 'Fun is the one thing that money can't buy . . . Something inside that was always denied for so many years.'[39] Whether it was Lennon or McCartney who wrote the last two lines, by then both of them knew that fun is not the only, nor even the most important, commodity that money can't buy: money can't buy you love.

27

The world could be ending if rock 'n' roll is playing. It's a disease of mine. [40]

Quarry Men

In January 1956, when John was 15, Lonnie Donegan of the Chris Barber Jazz Band hit the UK charts with his jaunty version of 'Rock Island Line', a classic country blues song of the American railroad, written by Leadbelly. It was the first 'skiffle' hit, and the first record that John Lennon ever bought, a fragile 78 rpm single. It kickstarted his musical career.

A spin-off from early American jazz with an infectious beat and a hillbilly accent, skiffle was the latest sensation in Britain. Though it spawned surprisingly few chart successes, after 'Rock Island Line' literally thousands of skiffle groups sprang up. There were said to be 500 in Liverpool alone. Similar phenomena have been fairly frequent since then – the punk, grunge, garage and rap explosions, for example – but in the 1950s this was something quite new, a signal of modern youth's psychological independence from the previous generation, which was still emotionally dominated by the aftermath of World War Two. Skiffle was noisy, untidy music that tended to annoy your parents, and it was not difficult to play: you had to master a few guitar or banjo chords, and someone had to be brave enough to sing, but otherwise all you needed was a washboard to run thimbles over, and a box bass made from an old tea-chest, a broom handle and some wire. If you could find a drummer with his own set of drums as well, you were doing well indeed.

John Lennon remembered that 'I then convinced my mother to buy me a "guaranteed not to split" guitar that we sent away for from one of those mail order firms. I suppose it was a bit crummy when you think about it, but I played it all the time and I got a lot of practice. She taught me banjo chords. If you look at early photos of the group you can see me playing funny chords. It's a joke in the family, "A guitar's all right John, but it can't earn you money."'[41]

Julia loved music. Some of the hits she heard with Freddie in the late 1920s and early 1930s would become favourites of John's too, like Gene Austin's 'Girl Of My Dreams' or 'Little White Lies', an Al Jolson number.[42] She had given John a toy guitar when he was four, before he had gone to Aunt Mimi's. Then when he came round to the house she taught him to play Ben E. King's 'Stand By Me' on her banjo. After that she got him the Spanish guitar, a three-quarter sized Gallotone Champion flat top acoustic, costing £10. (In 1999 it would sell at Sotheby's for £140,000.) Using the banjo as reference, she tuned the guitar's top four strings to G, set the bottom two to the same note as the fourth, and taught John to play Buddy Holly's 'That'll Be The Day'. In a little while he had mastered 'Rock Island Line' as well. Not to be outdone, Aunt Mimi soon afterwards bought him a better one for about £17.

And a few months later, John felt confident enough to start his own skiffle group, called the Black Jacks. Cannily, a week later he changed the name to the Quarry Men, after the school anthem which began 'Quarry Men, strong before our birth'. Thus honoured, the school gritted its teeth and allowed the group to gain experience on the stage of the assembly hall from time to time, which culminated in an unpaid spot during the interval of the Sixth Form Ball. Slowly, they improved.

After 'Rock Island Line', the next record John bought was Elvis Presley's new single, 'Hound Dog', released in Britain in September 1956. This was not skiffle, but rock 'n' roll. With its enigmatic and possibly obscene lyrics, its driving beat, and Elvis's sexy, muttered delivery, the song

32

was a revelation to John. 'It was Elvis who really got me out of Liverpool. Once I heard it and got into it, that was life, there was no other thing. I thought of nothing else but rock 'n' roll; apart from sex and food and money – but that's all the same thing, really.'[43]

In the 1950s, the BBC had a radio monopoly in Britain. The only popular music station from 'Auntie Beeb',[44] as John called it, was the Light Programme, playing mostly middle-of-the-road material: standards, palm court orchestra arrangements, movie music and ballads by English or American crooners, with the occasional comedy song thrown in. Legend claims that the Beatles were inspired by obscure American records deposited by sailors in coffee shop jukeboxes, but in fact much of their early inspiration came from the listening booths of of good record shops like Epstein's North End Music Store (NEMS) and from Radio Luxembourg, then broadcasting from the mainland of Europe to a new generation of UK pop music fans. After John had heard Elvis, a crackling Luxembourg introduced him to the music of such rockers as Little Richard, Jerry Lee Lewis, Eddie Cochran and Gene Vincent, as well as to others whose more melodic style crossed the barrier between rock 'n' roll and country music, such as Carl Perkins and Buddy Holly (who wore spectacles like John's, even on stage, and became a particular hero.) The words of many of the numbers that the Quarry Men played were copied down on the wing from Radio Luxembourg. It was a practice that led to John's first exercises in coarse song writing: producing his own substitute lyrics for songs that he hadn't heard properly or couldn't remember.

In the late spring of 1957, Quarry Bank entered J W Lennon to sit for 'O' levels in nine subjects. He achieved the distinction of passing none, not even Art: 'We had one question which said do a picture of "travel". I drew a picture of a hunchback with warts all over him.'[45] That July, aged 16, he left school for the last time. Though Pete Shotton would mistakenly remember that William Pobjoy, the headmaster, had predicted on John's last report card:

'This boy is bound to fail',[46] in fact Pobjoy's endorsement contrived to be even more depressing: 'I believe he is not beyond redemption and he could really turn out a fairly responsible adult who might go far.'[47]

With no thought as yet of making a living through music, John needed money, and wondered vaguely about robbing a shop. Instead, however, he concocted a plan with Nigel Walley. They went down to the Liverpool Docks to enrol on the Seamen's Employment Register at the Pier Head. This would make them eligible for training as ships' restaurant stewards who, rumour had it, were paid a fortune. After the Registry official rang Aunt Mimi to check John's details, the application was refused, and the official warned that his aunt was on the warpath and wanted him home immediately. No doubt it did not escape Mimi that if John had been accepted he would have been following the wake of his wastrel of a father. By now, John could remember very little about Freddie Lennon – though Pete Shotton reports that at around this time Freddie was in Manchester and tried to contact his son; when the proposed meeting failed to happen, John was apparently deeply upset.

Possibly the reunion was sabotaged by Mimi, who was now desperately worried that John would end up like 'that Alf' Lennon: 'At the back of my mind I was thinking of his father and how he had turned out, but of course I could never say that to John,' she would later admit.[48] The world of the teenage boy was alien territory for her. She had recently discovered sexy verses under John's pillow, and last year had to throw out a lot of his disgusting papers. ('One day I'll be famous and you're going to regret it,' he had said.[49] Mimi doubted it very much indeed.) Now she was discovering other suspect writings in his bedroom, but they were written so badly that she couldn't read them at all. John seemed to be getting worse and worse every day. With his drainpipe trousers and the coloured shirts that Julia was giving him, he was turning into a Teddy boy from the Liverpool slums. Smoking. Drinking. Those sideboards, and the hair. And as for that terrible skiffle . . .

'I come from the macho school of pretence,' John would say in 1980. 'I was never really a street kid or a tough guy. I used to dress like a Teddy boy and identify with Marlon Brando and Elvis Presley, but I was never really in any street fights or down-home gangs. I was just a suburban kid, imitating the rockers. But it was a big part of one's life to look tough. I spent the whole of my childhood with shoulders up around the top of me head and me glasses off because glasses were sissy, and walking in complete fear, but with the toughest-looking little face you've ever seen.'[50]

For most of the inhabitants of England, 6 July 1957 was just one more of those long English Saturdays in high summer whose details sooner or later fade away into oblivion. In the green and pleasant parish of Woolton, however, the events of the day can still be traced with some clarity. Against all the odds, it was about to enter history.

St Peter's Parish Church was holding its annual garden fête, with proceeds from entrance tickets, stalls and a hired funfair going to church funds. A programme of the event survives: festivities are to commence at two pm with a procession through the village, led by the Band of the Cheshire Yeomanry. In the Church Field at three o'clock, after her husband has declared the fête open, Mrs Thelwall Jones officiates at the Crowning of the Rose Queen, to be followed by a Fancy Dress Parade for children. A Display by the City of Liverpool Police Dogs takes place at 5.15. For most of the afternoon the Cheshire Yeomanry will continue playing 'Musical Selections', though at 4.15 and 5.45 pm the Quarry Men Skiffle Group will entertain the younger elements of the crowd. The climax of the fête, a Grand Dance in the Church Hall at eight o'clock, will feature the George Edwards Band, with the very hardworking Quarry Men skiffling again as support act.

The Woolton fête was the first paid public engagement that the Quarry Men had landed, though they had appeared before (usually for nothing) at birthdays, weddings and street parties, and also at St Peter's Youth Club (where a faulty microphone had once made John walk off in a fury.) The group's line-up had been in almost constant flux since the beginning, but today there were six of them on the outdoor stage. John Lennon was lead singer and lead guitarist. Eric Griffiths played rhythm guitar, and Rod Davis had a banjo. Len Garry (somewhat unwillingly) struggled with a tea-chest bass. Percussion was supplied by Colin Hanton on a 'Broadway' drum kit, which he was buying on hire purchase, and by Pete Shotton, scraping and hammering away at his mother's washboard. Bessie Shotton had been letting the Quarry Men practise in the old air raid shelter in her back garden, and it was she who had talked the rector into engaging them for the fête. With the terrible Lennon and Shotton involved, his agreement was a tribute both to Bessie's powers of persuasion and to old Prycee's Christian charity.

The ceremonial cavalcade that afternoon around the sunny streets and lanes of Woolton and up the hill to the Church Field had been embarrassing for the Quarry Men. At the head of the procession marched the 25 musical Yeomen, blowing and pounding their instruments, followed by packs of Cubs, Brownies, Girl Guides and Morris Dancers, and a gaggle of children in fancy dress. Five decorated flatbed lorries carried displays and more participants. On the last of these, a coal truck, the Quarry Men were perched on kitchen chairs. They had been told to play as they travelled, and managed to hammer out a song or two, but as they rolled along, shaking and rattling, it was impossible to be heard above the brass band ahead. Later, when John had set up properly on stage with the group around him, the Tannoy at full volume, the microphone on and a generally appreciative audience in front of him, things began to go very much better . . .

'I was having a cup of tea in the refreshment tent,' Aunt Mimi remembered. 'Suddenly, in the midst of everything, came this – this eruption of noise. Everyone had drained away from where I stood, into the next door field. And there on the stage I saw them – John and that Shotton. John saw me standing there with my mouth open. He started

Right-handed Lennon and left-handed McCartney: when they composed together in the early days, it was 'like looking into a mirror'

to make words up about me in the song he was singing. "Mimi's coming," he sang. "Oh, oh, Mimi's coming down the path.""[51] As she advanced towards the noise, she was appalled to see her nephew yelling fit to bust, with a horrid shirt on (but not his glasses). 'It was the first time I saw him with others playing,' she would say. 'It was a bombshell and a shock. I had no idea he would be there. It was forced home to me that day that I had been fighting a losing battle. Even then I would not give in. What a waste of my life and, more important, my health.'[52]

That morning John had left the house without saying a word to her about anything. But news of his impending performance that afternoon had been spreading around the area. Cousin Stan, Aunt Harrie and Aunt Nannie turned up to see what was going on. Geoff Rhind from school came along with his camera, and took his famous photograph of the Quarry Men on stage. Julia Lennon was there too, of course, with both her daughters. Ivan Vaughan, one of the original 'Outlaws', even brought along a friend of his to meet John, a 15-year-old boy from Allerton called Paul McCartney, who arrived with a guitar slung over his shoulder.

Participants and witnesses have disagreed about which songs the Quarry Men performed at Woolton fête that day. John thought he remembered doing Gene Vincent's 1956 hit, 'Be Bop A Lula', and 'Bony Maronie' by Larry Williams. Paul noticed him 'improving' the words to 'Come Go With Me', a song by the Del-Vikings. Other numbers said to have been played that day include Lonnie Donegan's 'Railroad Bill' and 'Cumberland Gap', and a version of a bawdy Liverpool song, 'Maggie Mae' (of which a snatch may be heard on the Beatles' last album, 'Let it Be'). One visitor, Bob Molyneux, was so impressed by the group's afternoon sessions that he rushed home to get his tape recorder. That evening at the 'Grand Dance', he captured John Lennon's voice on tape, apparently for the first time, singing Donegan's 'Puttin' on the Style' and Elvis's 'Baby Let's Play House'.

While the Quarry Men were moving their equipment into the Church Hall for the evening stint, Ivan Vaughan wandered in with Paul McCartney and introduced him. Paul was younger than they were, and the conversation was a bit awkward as they were all drinking beer, so without much prompting he played them Eddie Cochran's 'Twenty Flight Rock'. Then he did his party piece, a medley of Little Richard's hits that could almost have been the great man himself if you shut your eyes. John was impressed. The lad might be young, but obviously he was into the right music. He could sing and play as well as any of the Quarry Men, and he looked like Elvis Presley. John discussed the matter with Pete over the next few days.

When Paul was next spotted in Woolton, he was invited to join the group. He accepted as nonchalantly as he could. From now on John and Paul spent as much time as possible together, practising in the McCartney sitting-room when Paul's dad was out, or in the tile and glass porch of Mendips with its jangling acoustics, or in Julia's bathroom, another spectacular soundbox, where she taught them more songs from her youth, standards such as 'Ramona' and 'Wedding Bells'. The other Quarry Men were a little wary of the new boy, who liked to give the impression that he was quietly confident of his own abilities; there was some satisfaction during his inaugural appearance on stage with them in October, when Paul badly fluffed a lead solo and announced afterwards that, no, thank you, he didn't want to be their lead guitarist after all, and would stick to rhythm guitar if they didn't mind. Later that evening Paul consoled himself by playing for John a song he had written, his first composition, called 'I Lost My Little Girl'. Impressed, John went home and in immediate response wrote his own first song, the more optimistic 'Hello Little Girl'. Though Buddy Holly (one of the few rockers who also wrote his own material) might have claimed royalties on the middle section, John's song was the more impressive debut of the two, a little word-heavy perhaps, but with an attractive tune. It would still be in the Beatles' repertoire four years later.

The Lennon-McCartney pattern had begun. John had always worked best in partnership – he was naturally extremely lazy, and needed the immediate stimulus of an audience to get him to do anything at all. During his school career, Pete Shotton had supplied him with the necessary uncritical appreciation, but Paul's position was a greater challenge. John was aware that Paul was more musically intuitive than he was, with a better grasp of important matters like harmony and a more versatile singing voice, but he still had to prove that he was any good on stage. Paul was very young, and as the Quarry Men's founder John was well able to defend his position as leader. However, the tension between the pair impelled them continually to raise the stakes, both as performers and composers. It would be one of the crucial factors that drove the Beatles (inevitably, it now seems) towards 'the toppermost of the poppermost',[53] as John's much quoted mantra of encouragement was soon to put it.

Feeling left out, the other Quarry Men were deserting the group one after another. After John joshingly smashed the washboard over his head Pete withdrew in good heart to join the Police Force. Others stormed off after arguments about payment, or moaning about how they were being treated as part-time session musicians, wheeled out only on the rare occasions when John managed to get a booking for what was left of the group. Then Paul mentioned a fellow he knew from his school (the Liverpool Institute, in Mount Street), who wasn't a bad guitarist, though he was very young. In March 1958, after hearing the little chap play Bill Justis's 'Raunchy' for him on the top deck of a bus, John rather doubtfully agreed to try him out as a Quarry Man. Since he had already been in a group, he might find know someone with gigs for them. George Harrison was later to comment, 'I remember going to John's house once, soon after we met. I was still at the Institute and I looked a bit young. We were trying to look like Teddy boys – and I must have looked pretty good, because Mimi didn't like me at all. She was really shocked and said, "Look at him! Why have you brought this boy round to my house? He looks dreadful, like a Teddy boy." And he'd say, "Shut up, Mary, shut up." So he would come round to my house a lot and my mother would give us little glasses of whisky.'[54]

John, Paul and George became the core of the new Quarry

Men. Soon, performing on stage had become almost routine. As their musical skills and repertoire improved, they worked hard on the American-style harmonies that would later become characteristic of the Beatles' sound. The results of their labours so far were preserved on a single shellac 78 that they recorded on a portable disc cutting machine in early July 1958. The A side was a cover version of 'That'll Be The Day', Buddy Holly's hit from the previous September; it was backed by a song written by Paul and George, called 'In Spite Of All The Danger'. Though in later years each of the Beatles normally took the lead on their own songs, John, still emphatically the group's main vocalist, sang lead on both tracks, by no means badly.

On 15 July 1958, three days after making the record, John was in Julia's house with Bobby Dykins and his little sisters, waiting for his mother to come home after visiting Mimi at Mendips. The doorbell rang. It was a policeman, and he had terrible news. Julia Lennon had been knocked down by a car and killed as she crossed the dual carriageway of Menlove Avenue. John's mother was dead. 'It was the worst thing that ever happened to me. We'd caught up so much, me and Julia, in just a few years. We could communicate . . . . I thought "Fuck it, fuck it, fuck it. That's really fucked everything. I've no responsibilities to anyone now."'[55] After the ordeal of the funeral, John's cousin Leila took him, as she recalled, 'back to my home, The Cottage, and John and I just sat there on the couch, him with his head on my lap. I never said a word. We were both numb with anguish.'[56] For John the Quarry Men were no longer worth bothering with any more – the group would not meet again for months. The only copy of the first Lennon-McCartney record was shoved to the back of a drawer and forgotten. It could easily have been the last. More than twenty years were to pass before it would be played again, when John's voice would once more be heard singing its opening words:

> That'll be the day when you say goodbye,
> That'll be the day when you make me cry,
> You say you're gonna leave, you know it's a lie,
> That'll be the day when I die.

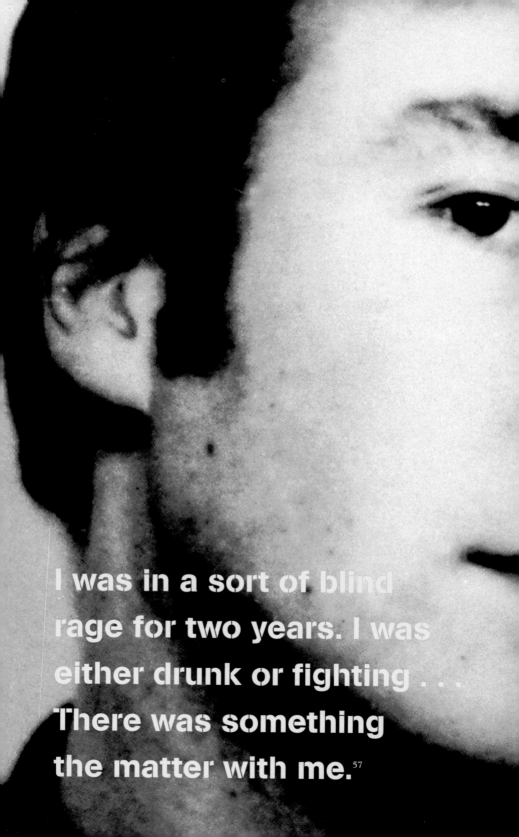

I was in a sort of blind
rage for two years. I was
either drunk or fighting . . .
There was something
the matter with me.[57]

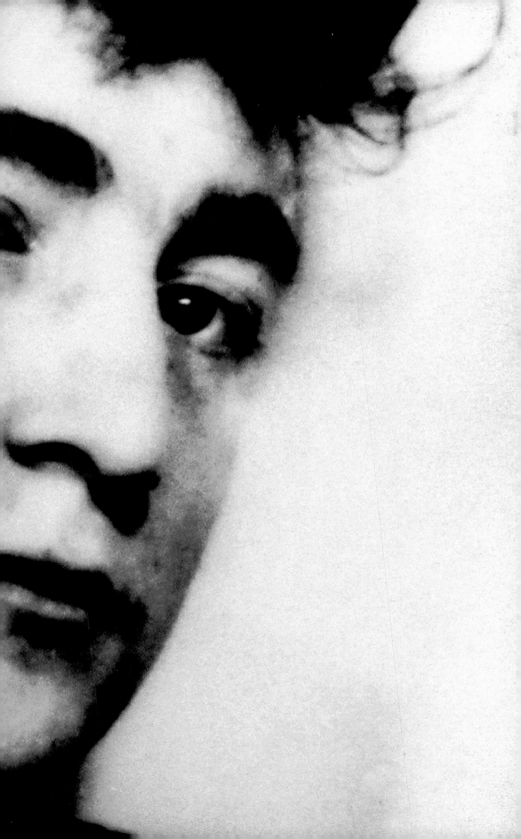

It Won't Be Long[58]

When Julia died, John had already been an art student for almost a year. Hoping that it might get him to focus on something less foolish than skiffle, Mimi had visited Pobjoy at Quarry Bank and somehow persuaded him to recommend her nephew for Liverpool Art College. After a plausible interview, to which he brought only a sheaf of cartoons and some caricatures of Quarry Bank teachers, John had been given a place there, on the intermediate course. This offered an introduction to all aspects of art for the first two years, followed by two further years working on a single chosen subject. He began in the autumn of 1957. John fancied that the life of a bohemian artist would suit him very nicely.

'They all thought I was a Ted at art college when I arrived. Then I became a bit artier, as they all do, but I still dressed like a Ted, in black with tight drainies.'[59] With his caustic manner and menacing clothes to match, from the outset John was treated with nervous suspicion by many of the tutors. To confirm their prejudices he began to disrupt classes by turning up flamboyantly late, sitting in the nude model's lap and producing an interesting range of schoolboy noises. As a result he was barred from the painting school, which he had looked forward to, and was assigned instead to the lettering class, a discipline whose primary goals were accuracy and tidiness. 'They might as well have put me in sky-diving.'[60] Nor, as it turned out, were the architecture, perspective and geometrical drawing or anatomy classes any more suited to his talents: during his years in the college he was to learn almost nothing about technique. His only advocate among the staff was a maverick lecturer, Arthur Ballard, a celebrated abstract painter and heroic drinker, who was impressed by a notebook full of John's caricatures and illustrated verses that he found lying around. At one point Ballard intervened to stop him being ejected from the college for gross laziness. He claimed to be able to discern a glimmer of talent through John's disguises, which now included foul language and broad Scouse vowels to go with the Teddy boy gear: 'I think Lennon put it on. He had quite a posh accent at the time by Liverpool standards.'[61] Ballard was never to forget coming across John one day, sitting alone in a window of the College, in tears. 'If I had my way he would never have been a Beatle,' he said later, 'he would have been a professional artist.'[62]

While John's academic achievements were difficult to pinpoint, his extracurricular activities were more conspicuous. During his first year in College, the Quarry Men's few official appearances were at venues like the illegal Morgue Skiffle Cellar, but more often they held impromptu concerts in the canteen or in Room 21, an empty classroom which John invaded for rehearsals. After Julia was killed, however, this all came to an end, and his energies were directed elsewhere. 'If you go to my art school and ask about my career there, it was mainly being drunk.'[63] Whether he was displaying his Teddy boy persona or its successor, the enigmatic Beat Poet look (which allowed him to wear his black-rimmed spectacles), everyone noticed John Lennon when he was on the booze. The Liverpool poet Adrian Henri, an inveterate early Lennon-watcher, spotted him 'swimming' along the floor of Ye Cracke, the student pub in Rice Street. As an apprentice member of the Beat Generation, he showed no interest in money, quickly spending the 30 shillings that Mimi gave him per week, and then bumming off his friends.

Drunk or sober, John liked to shock with his humour, which was now sicker than ever. 'He could be very cruel. Walking down the street he would go "Boo" in front of old people. And if he saw anyone who was crippled or deformed, he'd make loud remarks, like "Some people will do anything to get out of the army,"' recalls Thelma Pickles, a soulmate and occasional bedmate at this time. 'He used to do a lot of cruel drawings. I thought they were marvellous. He did one of some women cooing over some babies, saying weren't they lovely. All the babies were deformed, with hideous faces.'[64]

Hand in hand with the drink, came the women. From his earliest years, John had already been much more sexually active than Mimi could have dreamed. He had begun spectacularly at primary school, pouncing on girls and pulling their knickers down. While at Quarry Bank he used to climb over the wall into Calderstones Girls' School, hoping for what he called 'Experience Lessons',[65] though history does not relate how successful these daring missions were. Pete Shotton's curiously detailed memoir describes, perhaps too graphically, the young Lennon's enthusiastic exploration of his seething teenage sexuality, specifically with a girl called Barbara Baker. David Ashton, another schoolboy acquaintance and Lennon chronicler, attempts discretion, but manages to make his account even more suggestive by remembering that local girls at the time refused to tell him details of John's carnal encounters: 'If you knew what we know you would not like him.' Ashton then goes on to list the places around Woolton where such encounters would have taken place – the 'dark lane and graveyard of St Mary's Catholic Church, St Peter's Church Field or lane going up to it, The Mill Style, Strawberry Fields Grounds, Woolton Woods and Out Lane'.[66]

So it was that Barbara and Thelma, and undoubtedly

quite a number of others, had already come and gone by the end of 1958, when at a College Christmas party John got together with a fellow art student named Cynthia Powell, from across the Mersey in middle-class Cheshire. He hadn't considered her at first: 'She was a right Hoylake runt. Dead snobby. "Quiet please," we'd shout. "No dirty jokes. It's Cynthia."'[67] At first she seemed too prim for a hard man like Lennon, but he talked her into bed quickly enough, and after he had persuaded her to dye her hair and wear short skirts like his favourite pin-up, Brigitte Bardot, he allowed her to become part of his life. Sometimes he would sit with her in the pub, holding her hand all evening. John was never easy to be with, however. 'I was pretty self-destructive . . . when I went to art school in Liverpool, you know, it was mainly one long drinking session . . . I remember at college I always got a little violent on drink . . . punching through telephone box glass . . . a kind of self-destructive suicide side of me . . .'[68] It was not only telephone boxes. Cynthia was frightened of John's unpredictable rages, and with good reason. He used to hit her, hard: 'I was jealous of anyone she had anything to do with. I demanded absolute trust from her, just because I wasn't trustworthy myself.'[69] The lines John contributed in 1967 to the song 'Getting Better' referred, as he would later point out, directly to himself: 'I used to be cruel to my woman, I beat her and kept her apart from the things that she loved . . .'[70]

New Year's Day 1959 was the first time that the Quarry Men got together for money since Julia's death almost six months before. The occasion was a party for the Speke Bus Depot Social Club, where the chairman, Harold Harrison (George's father), had recommended them for the booking. As his parents were present George avoided the free beer on offer, but John and Paul knocked back as many pints as they could. The pair were in fine form after the interval, teasing George in front of everyone about his laborious guitar solos, and rudely mocking the indignant theatre manager's stage make-

48

up as he tried to reason with them. The evening was a fiasco, and almost finished off the Quarry Men: despite having been blind drunk himself, Colin Hanton left the group that night, taking his valuable drum kit with him. Even George gave John and Paul up as a bad job and was soon perfecting his solos as an occasional member of the Les Stewart Quartet. By 3 February, when news came of Buddy Holly's death in a plane crash, John's interest in music-making seemed already to be a thing of the past. After the end of that second year at Art College, he found summer work as a labourer at the Scaris and Brick Water Works. (Apart from some temporary hotel work in his teens with Bobby Dykins, this was the only conventional job that John would ever have.) He clocked up four weeks before being sacked on 28 August as 'unsuitable'. A day later, however, John Lennon would begin to play his music again. It was all thanks to George Harrison.

By 1959 the skiffle craze was over. Most of the outfits in Liverpool had either broken up or mutated into beat groups with lineups of electric guitars, bass and drums, who played rock 'n' roll or country & western, plus some of the latest hits, to young audiences in suburban halls and coffee clubs. In August 1959 the latest of these clubs, the Casbah, needed a group at very short notice, as the Les Stewart Quartet, which had been engaged for its opening night, had suddenly imploded. George seized the opportunity and volunteered the Quarry Men, and Mona Best, the Casbah's proprieter, agreed to engage John, Paul and George to play one night a week, despite their lack of both bass player and drums. If anyone asked them where their drummer was, they just bluffed it out: 'The rhythm's in the guitars.'[71] It was no bad thing: the extra energy that they had to inject into their playing at the Casbah gave the group its first real fans. Cynthia faithfully attended every performance, sitting for hours in front of the stage with a microphone lashed to a broom handle for John to sing into. The eight weeks' residency helped in one other important way: their appearance fee was enough to allow John and George to buy their first electric guitars. Perhaps seeing a gap in the market, Pete Best, Mona's son, bought a drum kit at around this time too, and began to teach himself to play.

With the new guitars, came renewed ambition. The Quarry Men now became Johnny and the Moondogs, following the usual pattern for Liverpool beat group names: among their hundreds of rivals were Ritchie and the Galvanisers, Rocky Stone and the Pebbles and the renowned Rikki and the Red Streaks. The days of tea-chests were over, and they needed a proper electric bass player if they were to be contenders, but none of the three existing Moondogs wanted to play it, and besides, the instrument cost over £50, an impossible sum. Or so it seemed. However, John's closest friend at Art College, Stuart Sutcliffe, had just sold his first painting for £65: John invited him to join his band if he bought a bass guitar. There was of course the minor matter of learning how to play it. John assured Stuart that he would pick it up in no time: audiences never listened to the bass line, anyway. Perhaps at first he could stand sideways on stage, and then nobody would be able to see what his fingers were up to. And so, in January 1960, Stuart became a Moondog too.

John admired his friend both for his style and his application. Stuart Sutcliffe was a real artist, an abstract expressionist with a studio (really just a rented room in a house) in Gambier Terrace close to Liverpool Cathedral. He took his work seriously. Adrian Henri later took the view that John followed Stuart around, 'the way Prince Philip follows the Queen.'[72] To an outsider, it might have seemed so, but then Her Majesty is hardly the butt of incessant teasing from the Duke of Edinburgh: John's barbs were part of their relationship. At least some of his minor cruelties had the excuse of being witty: when Stuart proudly produced a new painting for his scrutiny, John simply commented, 'Hanging's too good for it.'[73]

The pair would spend hours in Ye Cracke talking

about artists that Stuart liked, often as much for their dissipated or otherwise blighted lives as for their work. During these discussions John learned about Van Gogh, Gauguin, Modigliani, the Surrealists and the Dadaists, figures who helped John to understand aspects of himself, as he would later explain: 'Surrealism had a great effect on me because then I realized that the imagery in my mind wasn't insanity – that if it was insane, then I belonged to an exclusive club that sees the world in those terms. Surrealism to me is reality. Psychedelic vision is reality to me and always was. When I looked at myself in the mirror at twelve, thirteen – when you become very conscious as a teenager of your appearance, and spend a lot of time combing your hair – I used to, literally, trance out into alpha . . . I would find myself seeing these hallucinatory images of my face changing, becoming cosmic and complete.'[74]

The friendship worked in both directions. Stuart found in John an example of what he himself was preaching but did not quite dare to practice. John's sharp, untutored mind despised any form of authority and even tried to avoid the tyranny of rational logic. He formed his ideas and his art, such as it was, from anything he happened to find lying around, allowing chance, the random, to do much of the work for him, and then 'Lennonizing' the results with black humour. Thus, the graphic work he produced tended to consist of semi-parodic images, executed with the minimum of technical care; the same would go for almost all his prose and verse from the *Daily Howl* onwards. In even the simplest of his early songs John would often subtly alter the usual formulaic conventions of the three-minute hymn to love by adding a hint of the subversive, while much of his later music would seem consciously to avoid the fripperies of coherence and sometimes even of melody. John's invitation to Stuart Sutcliffe to join the group was itself a direct result of this 'philosophy of the arbitrary'; his friend simply happened to be hanging around with the necessary money in his pocket, like an *objêt trouvée*. Stuart's lack of discernable musical ability might therefore even prove an advantage in the end, and besides, he would look cool on stage in his black gear and sunglasses. Another, more important, reason why John asked him to join the group was because Stuart was his best mate, he loved him, and he wanted to keep him in his life.

John was now using Mimi's house largely as a refuelling station for food, laundry, money and occasionally sleep, as he had taken up unofficial residence with Stuart in Gambier Terrace. In July he would be seen there, lying on the floor, in a photograph published in the *Sunday People* to illustrate a feature oddly entitled 'The Beatnik Horror, for though they don't know it they are on the road to hell.'[75] (The article, supposedly exposing the vicious lifestyle of overeducated modern youth, began the later myth that John Lennon liked to sleep in a coffin.) Stuart proved to be useful to John in other ways too. As an active member of the Students' Union, he and the enthusiastic Bill Harry, budding journalist and already advocate of what one day he would dub the 'Mersey Sound,' persuaded the Committee to buy a new public address system and tape recorder for student events. Within a few weeks all this equipment had been commandeered by the Moondogs. It would never be returned.

About three months later, the purloined tape recorder was to capture a rare surviving example of Stuart's bass playing. The recording, which took place in Paul's father's sitting room, is of the worst quality, but on a slow instrumental by Paul called 'Cayenne', Stuart can be heard quite clearly, each note very far apart. On the same tape is a much more entertaining parody number in the style of the Ink Spots, called 'You'll Be Mine', probably an early Lennon-McCartney composition. Speaking in Goonishly lugubrious tones over the middle section, John makes a spoken declaration of love: 'My darling, when you brought me that toast the other morning, I . . . I looked into your eyes, and I could see your National Health eyeball, and I loved you like I've never done . . . I

52

have never done before.'[76] (There is of course no trace of the trademark 'Beatle' Scouse accent.)

One of John's early heroes and models, the crippled Gene Vincent, gave an affecting performance in a show in Liverpool on 3 May. Even Vincent's presence was heroic, since he had sustained further injuries three weeks before in the car crash that killed Eddie Cochran. The event was organized by Larry Parnes, a cigar-flourishing music impresario from London. Parnes was a big cheese, famous for his assertively rechristened stars, such as Billy Fury, Marty Wilde and Tommy Steele. Various local bands had been hastily recruited to fill the Cochran-shaped gap in the bill, though frustratingly not Johnny and the Moondogs, who had to buy tickets to hear their idol sing 'Be Bop A Lula'.

The next day John approached a minor local promoter, Allan Williams, asking him to act as agent for his group and get them some work. Williams, a convivial little Welshman, accepted with certain reservations, one of which was their terrible name. Stuart had suggested the 'Beetles', along the lines of Buddy Holly's backing group, the Crickets. John said that as they were a beat group, it should be spelt 'Beatals'. Williams liked none of these ideas, and finally settled on 'Long John and the Silver Beetles'. He also produced a drummer, Tommy Moore, who joined the group at once. (Tommy a stolid individual aged 36, did not particularly appreciate being called 'Dad' by John, and thought him 'big-headed and aggressive'[77].) As good as his word, their new manager soon found the group some work, and so they spent the next few days decorating the ladies' toilet at the Jacaranda Coffee Bar in Slater Street (Proprieter: Allan Williams). If they did that job properly, there might well be more interesting ones to follow.

I was raised in Liverpool, but I grew up in Hamburg.[78]

Getting Better [79]

John had been entering his band for talent competitions and auditions since the earliest days of the Quarry Men. He had twice tried Carroll Levis' Mr Star-Maker Talent Show, but without success. (Paul later remembered that they always seemed to be beaten by a fat lady who played the spoons.) At the Gene Vincent concert, Larry 'Parnes, Shillings and Pence', as he was rudely called in Liverpool, had been impressed by the city's many young groups, which nobody from London had noticed before. He returned later in May to choose one to back Billy Fury on a tour. At the audition, Fury himself chose the Silver Beetles – as they were now called, since 'Long John' was tired of the jokes. Unfortunately, Allan Williams, who was doubling as Parnes' man in Liverpool, told John that he would have to get rid of their incompetent bass player before he, as their manager, would let them go on the tour. John turned him down flat, and was sent away with a flea in his ear. Then, much to everyone's surprise, Parnes offered the group a nine day tour of the north of Scotland. They would be paid £18 each to back another of his singers, Johnny Gentle. Two days later, they were all on the train, professionals at last.

When they reached Alloa and met Johnny Gentle, John told him excitedly: 'This is our big break. We've been waiting for this!'[80] But the tour turned out to be a badly

57

organized shambles, chiefly memorable for a road accident that sent a guitar smashing into Tommy Moore's face and put him in hospital with concussion. Not for long, however: John dragged him out of bed to play that night, gap-toothed and swathed in bandages. Within two weeks of getting home Tommy had given up drumming forever to begin a new career at the Garston bottle-works.

Though they had been disappointed by their week in Scotland, things began to improve in Liverpool. Their new manager had got them several more gigs while they were away, and for the first time it looked as if it might just be possible one day to earn a living this way. They were to play a dozen times or so in the Jacaranda, and also became regulars at the Institute in Neston and the Grosvenor Ballroom, Wallasey. Both these venues were magnets for rival Teddy boy gangs from Bootle and Garston, and scenes of drunken violence were liable to erupt without warning. On 11 June 'a Liverpool rhythm group' called 'The Beatles' received its first mention in a local newspaper, complete with exotic stagenames: 'John Lennon, the leader, plays one of the three rhythm guitars, the other guitarists being Paul Ramon and Carl Harrison. Stuart da Stael plays the bass, and the drummer is Thomas Moore.'[81] John seems to have recognized that the group had passed an important milestone: he had no longer any intention of ever returning to Art College – though he did not say so to Mimi.

Gerry and the Pacemakers, also trying to make a name in Liverpool, at least once shared a bill with the Beatles in the terrifying Grosvenor Ballroom. 'Their sound was rubbish,' Gerry Marsden remembered, 'but [Paul] and John stood out as talented. Somehow whatever John did was just "different". He seemed to have absorbed all the rock 'n' roll influences and then come out the other side with entirely his own variation on them.'[82] One factor that made John different was that he had been absorbing not just rock 'n' roll, but the original black American music from which it had sprung, known as 'Rhythm and Blues' (which before the 1950s had been known as 'Race Music'.) R&B paradoxically combined its religious roots in gospel music with a slangy

58

appreciation of the delights of sexual congress, though later it would often be censored for white audiences who hardly knew what the offending terms meant anyway. In the words of Little Richard, 'Rhythm and blues had a baby, and they called it rock 'n' roll.'[83] The frenzy that accompanied his performances was one of the factors that propelled R&B into the mainstream, clearing the way for Presley and others to follow. Purists have sometimes felt (and anyone watching Chubby Checker singing 'Rock Around The Clock' might be forced to agree) that rock 'n' roll was merely a sanitized version of R&B. John Lennon used the term, however, to cover all the black music that first inspired him, from Big Joe Turner and Ruth Brown to Ray Charles and Arthur Alexander, as well as harmony-rich groups like the Coasters, the Drifters, the Isley Brothers and the Shirelles. In 1973, he recalled his early influences: 'we felt very exclusive and underground in Liverpool listening to all those old time records. And nobody was listening to any of them except Eric Burdon in Newcastle and Mick Jagger in London. It was that lonely. It was fantastic.'[84] In fact the Beatles were far from the only British bands picking up on Rhythm and Blues at the time – news of good music travels fast. By the early 1960s even Cliff Richard and the Shadows were doing once obscure R&B titles, including, unlikely as it may seem, 'Willie And The Hand Jive' by Johnny Otis.

There were more appearances. In July the Beatles found themselves clad in matching lilac jackets in an illegal 'Artistes Club', earning ten shillings a night to play Duane Eddy's 'Ramrod' behind a stripper called Janice. The experience did little to prepare them, however, for what lay ahead among the mean streets of Hamburg, where after a series of accidents, Allan Williams had got them a residency at the Indra Club, in the justifiably named Grosse Freiheit ('Great Freedom') area of the city. They would be earning £15 a week or so (though to shut Mimi up John told her it would be £100). But without a drummer they wouldn't be able to go, until someone remembered Mona Best's son in the Casbah. 'We had all sorts of drummers all the time, because people

George Harrison, Stuart Sutcliffe and John taken by Jürgen Vollmer during their first photoshoot in Hamburg

who owned drum kits were few and far between. It was an expensive item. They were usually idiots. Then we got Pete Best because we needed a drummer to go to Hamburg the next day. Allan Williams took us over in a van. We went through Holland and we did a bit of shoplifting there.'[85]

They were given two windowless concrete rooms behind the screen in the nearby *Bambi-Filmkunsttheater* to sleep in, and on 17 August 1960 began the first of 48 nights at the Indra. Every evening they were expected to be on stage from 7.30 pm until after two in the morning, with two or three half-hour breaks allowed. It was very tough. Initially, their employer, Bruno Koschmider, was unhappy with their performance, telling them, as John recalled: '"The first night you were terrible, you have to make a show – mak show." So, I put my guitar down and I did Gene Vincent all night, you know, banging and lying on the floor, and throwing the mike around, and pretending that I had a bad leg. . . . I played fucking Gene Vincent for three weeks.'[86]

German nightclub life was very different from the ballroom circuit at home, and required stamina. 'My voice began to hurt with the pain of singing.'[87] In Liverpool they used to play the same songs at each appearance, but here the long hours on stage stretched their repertoire to the utmost. They began to find ways to get around their limitations. Ray Charles's 'What'd I Say' became a standby: with multiple solos, ad-libbing and audience participation in the 'Heys' and 'Yeahs' they could apparently make the song chug along for an hour. John used to dance round like a gorilla, taking requests, teasing the punters, joking and generally doing his Art College act. They began to build up a following.

After complaints about the terrible racket they were making, in October the Beatles were told to bring their 'Hamburg stamp and yell'[88] music to the Kaiserkeller. This was a better venue which even boasted a piano, and for the next eight weeks they shared the bill with another Liverpool outfit, Rory Storm and the Hurricanes, most days playing twelve-hour sets turn and turn about with them. The Beatles lifted many new songs from the Hurricanes, and stole more from Tony Sheridan, a charismatic rock 'n' roller at the nearby Top Ten Club who was known as 'The Teacher', and whose style on stage John tried to emulate. One day, in a strange foretaste of things to come, the other Beatles left Pete and Stuart behind and went off with Ringo Starr, the Hurricanes' drummer, to a booth behind the railway station, where as a fourpiece, with Paul on bass, they cut a demo disc of standards together – 'Fever', 'Summertime', possibly 'September Song'. John, Paul and George were to see much more of the drummer, but not of the record, which Allan Williams would eventually lose in a pub.

During their five stays in Hamburg over the next three years, John and the other Beatles were to clock up about 800 hours on stage. It was a training they would never have had in Liverpool. But it was even more dangerous than the Neston Institute or the Grosvenor: here the waiters had to carry truncheons and flick-knives to keep control. Whenever John smelt English cigarettes he knew that British sailors were in the building, and that they were probably in for a fight. 'We'd always be drunk because all these gangsters would come in, like the local Mafia. They'd send a crate of champagne onstage, this imitation German champagne, and we had to drink it or they'd kill us. They'd say, "Drink it, and then do 'What'd I Say'." . . . I'd be lying on the stage floor behind the piano, drunk, while the rest of the group was playing. . . . It would be a far-out show now . . . eating and smoking and swearing and going to sleep on stage when you were tired.'[89]

John discovered that the only way to survive Hamburg nights was to take pills. 'The waiters gave you them . . . the pills and drink.'[90] The pills were 'speed', at first in the form of Preludin, a slimming tablet containing amphetamine, quite effective when mixed with alcohol. (Speed fell out of general recreational use with the arrival of trippier drugs like cannabis and LSD, though it would reappear in the 1990s as part of the recipe for Ecstasy.) Curiously, despite the lawlessness around them in Hamburg, 'Prello' or 'Prellies', with other uppers like Black Bombers and Purple Hearts, seem to be the only recreational drug they took much of in Germany. The Beatles' circle in Liverpool was remarkably drug-free at this time too – their only previous experience was after a teenage 'beat poet' called Royston Ellis persuaded them to accompany a recital in the Art College of his then startlingly gay verse; when John and the others followed his advice and chewed up the contents of Vick inhalers to

John photographed in the attic by Astrid Kircherr

extract the benzedrine, they had talked all night.

Details of the Beatles' Hamburg visits, what happened where, and when, and to whom, are unreliable, partly because of the Prellies, the cheap champagne or schnapps, and the lack of sleep, and partly because the desire to tell a good story sometimes clashes with a certain reticence about the excesses of youth. We are told by various sources that John Lennon goosestepped around the stage with a swastika on his cap, pissed on nuns from a rooftop and was pissed on by the Kaiserkeller's bouncer, cut up the clothes of Paul's latest conquest with a scissors, berated his audiences with phrases such as 'Bloody Krauts', 'Back to your tank', 'Fucking Nazis' and *'Heil Hitler'*,[91] watched George lose his virginity, sang in his underpants with a toilet seat around his neck, mugged an English sailor, wrote 'John Lennon, King of Prello'[92] on a photograph of himself, took a pig for a stroll along the Reeperbahn on a lead, came in close contact with transvestites, threw a plate of food at George on stage, caught the clap and read the Marquis de Sade. There is little reason to doubt that most of it is true.

The Marquis de Sade book was a present from Astrid Kircherr, who knew John's tastes. She and her two friends Klaus Voorman and Jürgen Vollmer were fashion students who had found the Kaiserkeller by chance, and brought groups of their fellow students to admire their extraordinary new discoveries. John liked this blond, elfin girl and her black leather gear, and there was a frisson, but it was Stuart who Astrid fell for, and the attraction was mutual. John, feeling excluded, for a while became hostile and nasty to both of them, but calmed down after realizing that his friendship with Stuart would not be threatened by any girlfriend. The 'Exis' (Existentialists), as John called the three, would have an incalculable effect on the group's future. Soon Jürgen and Astrid were taking their influential and now familiar black and white Hamburg photographs of the Beatles, sexy leather-clad figures against a background of urban decay, and stark, powerful portraits, often lit from the side. Later, Jürgen would persuade John and Paul to adopt their fringed hairstyle, which was now quite common on the Continent but still unknown in Britain. As the 'Beatle cut,' it would bring the group millions of pounds' worth of publicity in the years to come. Klaus Voorman, who would eventually buy Stuart's bass guitar and learn to play, was to remain a close friend of John's for life.

By early December the other Beatles, minus Stuart, who was now engaged to Astrid, had straggled home. They were miserable and penniless after a very unpleasant falling out with Bruno Koschmider, convincing details of which have never clearly emerged. John was the last to return. He too was broke and depressed, though at least he had now got his first really good guitar, a Rickenbacker 325, which he had bought in Hamburg. He went to ground for a time at Mimi's, seeing only Cynthia, to whom he had been writing, he would claim, 'the sexiest letters this side of Henry Miller. Forty pages long some of them.'[93] When he emerged to reconvene the group he discovered that Paul, who on his return had been sent down to the labour exchange by his father, was now working as a lorry driver's mate, having apparently given up the idea of a life in music. It wasn't too hard to bully him into continuing as a Beatle. With a temporary bassist, Charles Newby, to cover for Stuart, the group was welcomed back on stage by their old fans at the Casbah on 17 December. Then, just after Christmas, they played a stormer of a set in the tatty ballroom of Litherland Town Hall, and caused a sensation. Bob Wooler, a local disc jockey famous for his excruciating 'Woolerisms' ('Meet the beat that's reet for the feet'),[94] had got them the date. Bob was knocked out: 'They were stomping like hell and people were going mad. They went crazy for their closing number, which was Ray Charles' "What'd I Say".'[95] Hamburg, louche in cowboy boots and leathers, had come to Liverpool: 'Suddenly we were a wow. Mind you, 70 per cent of the audience thought that we were a German wow, but we didn't care about that. Even in Liverpool, people didn't know we were from Liverpool. They thought we were from Hamburg. They said, "Christ, they speak good English!" which we did, of course, being English. It was that evening that we really came out of our shell and let go. We stood there being cheered for the first time. That was when we began to think that we were good. It was only back in Liverpool that we realized the difference and saw what had happened to us while everyone else was playing Cliff Richard shit.'[96]

The stuff that screams
are made of [97]

What About Brian Epstein?⁹⁸

In Litherland Town Hall that night, promoter Brian Kelly posted his bouncers on the door of the Beatles' dressing room to stop other promoters booking them before he did. The extraordinary reaction of the crowd was a turning point for the group: a single short performance had made them hot properties. Over the next three months they would play almost 100 gigs in the Liverpool area, to ever more rapturous audiences. On Valentine's Night John was knocked over when dozens of girls rushed the stage wanting to kiss Paul.

Being so much in demand, the band urgently had to be put on a more efficient footing. Charles Newby went back to college in the New Year, and Paul reluctantly took over as permanent bass guitarist. Friends old and new rallied around. Neil Aspinall, an intimate of Pete Best and of his mother, picked up an old van, and became the Beatles' first employee, driving them to and from gigs for £1 a night. Mona Best worked hard to set up dates in jive halls round the city, while Bob Wooler, agog with enthusiasm, mentioned them to the management of the Cavern Club, a dingy basement venue in Mathew Street where he was DJ ('Guardian of the Grooves'⁹⁹). Even Allan Williams, still supposed to be the Beatles' agent, arranged a couple of appearances back at the Grosvenor.

John had played in the Cavern at least twice before, in

the days of the Quarry Men. Then it was strictly a venue for jazz, and on sufferance, skiffle, and despite repeated warnings, he had insisted on playing rock 'n' roll. Cheeky introductions – John Lennon: 'and now an old favourite by Fats Duke Ellington Leadbelly'[100] – had failed to turn 'Long Tall Sally' into jazz, and the group had not become regulars. John always hated jazz anyway: 'I think it's shit music. It never gets anywhere, never does anything, it's always the same. And it's followed by students in Marks and Spencer pullovers and all they do is drink pints of beer.'[101]

At lunchtime on 9 February 1961, Bob laid on a special event to welcome, rather late in the day, the Beatles back from Hamburg. It would be the first of 292 appearances on the Cavern's little stage. Their families had been invited, and two of John's aunts, Mimi and Nannie, were brought by Cousin Stan to see their disgraceful nephew in action. 'And now the Beetles will play for the Ants,'[102] announced the unstoppable Bob. Peering gingerly around 'this terrible place', when Mimi saw John she was horrified, and exploded: 'Get him out. Get him out. Tell him to come off the stage. He can't stay here.'[103]

The first television footage of the group would be filmed in the Cavern over 18 months later. It can be seen on the six CD video anthology of the Beatles, but the film somehow fails to recapture the sensory overload of the club as the Beatles filled its three writhing cellars, walls glistening with teen sweat, with their jangling, tumultuous music. Ray Coleman, for his biography of John Lennon, took field research to its logical conclusion by gingerly sniffing a leather jacket that a female fan had kept unwashed since her dancing days there, as a trophy of the Beatles.[104] The atmosphere bore a high sexual charge for both males and females, made even more potent for some by the youthful innocence of the shopgirls and schoolgirls clustering around the stage. Variously called by the group the 'Cement Mixers', the 'Wooden Tops' or the 'Beatlettes', their greatest thrill was to be bought a cup of coffee by John or given the eye by Paul or Pete.

But perhaps it is dear old Bob 'Big Beat' Wooler who best sums up the excitement of those times: 'If you walked into Mathew Street . . . you'd see a doorway with clouds of steam coming up. That was heat generated from the bodies of those youngsters down below. If you had to go in, it was like stepping into a hot bath and then you'd have to fight your way into the band room . . . The heat must have been 100 degrees and the kids used to come out of there and spill out onto the streets, but they were a picture of happiness . . . Condensation would drip down the walls and the noise was incredible. The Beatles' music was very animal-like. It was earthy and very impressive. They would smoke on stage and John would stick a cigarette under the strings at the top of his guitar.'[105]

At the end of March the band returned by boat and train to Hamburg for a 13-week stint, this time at the Top Ten Club, where they appeared with Tony Sheridan. The job had been arranged without the help of Allan Williams, so they refused to pay him the ten per cent of their earnings that he expected. This led to a final parting of the ways with Williams, who sent them a heated two-page letter that ended resoundingly: 'I could have sworn you were all decent lads that is why I pushed you when nobody wanted to hear you.'[106] (Curiously for a proud Welshman, he accused them of 'welshing' three times in as many paragraphs.) Williams would later give an entertaining version of events in his book called *The Man Who Gave The Beatles Away*, which John promptly renamed as *The Man Who Couldn't Give The Beatles Away*.[107]

In June Cynthia came out to Germany to visit John and was looked after by Astrid. He was happy to see her, though the visit may have been a little stressful as he had not been entirely celibate in Hamburg. A few days later, while performing with Tony Sheridan, the group was spotted by a friend of Bert Kaempfert, the orchestra leader and all-round music man. Kaempfert was still basking in the glow of his 'Wonderland By Night', a number one hit in America, and he got them to record seven tracks for his Polydor label, five with Sheridan on lead vocals, and one with John, a stirring rock 'n' roll treatment of a whimsical ditty from the 1920s, 'Ain't She Sweet'. The final cut was 'Cry For A Shadow', George and John's instrumental parody of Cliff Richard's backing band, the Shadows, whom John scorned. Both of these tracks can be heard on 'Anthology 1', and testify to the Beatles' new professionalism, with Paul's inventive bass playing, George's more confident leads, and on 'Ain't She Sweet', John's maturing voice, ragged and distinctive.

They left Germany with a recording contract with Kaempfert that would last until mid-1962. In August, a single of their rocked-up version of 'My Bonnie (Lies Over The Ocean)' backed by 'When The Saints Go Marching In', both sung by Sheridan, was released in Germany. This was John's first ever commercial appearance on record. However, his band was billed as 'The Beat Brothers', as the word 'Beatle' was apparently indistinguishable from a German slang term for 'small penis'. The single would reached No 32 in Germany, where Sheridan was the star he would never be at home in Britain.

At the beginning of 1961, John F Kennedy had been elected President of the USA. The nuclear scares of the cold war were at their height, and the Campaign for Nuclear Disarmament was on the march around Britain. Though the Beatles were billed in February as purveyors of 'The Atom Beat', a short-lived craze consisting of a great deal of heavy stamping, this was the extent of their involvement in the world of politics. At Art College, John had of course read the obligatory *Communist Manifesto*, and had laid down the law during heated political discussions with Bill Harry and others in Ye Cracke. Bill had tried to involve John, or indeed anyone else he met, in his proposal to put Liverpool on the radical map by founding a group of activists called 'The Dissenters', which would become a powerhouse of artistic and political ideas to transform the city, and perhaps even the world. But John Lennon, already a dissenter, had declined to join. However, being an avid reader of the papers, he kept himself informed about current affairs and always had an opinion. Soon, thanks to Bill, he was to become a columnist.

When John got back from Hamburg on 3 July, he found his old journalist pal trying to launch a newspaper aimed at a beat-hungry Liverpool, carrying gig ads and chat about music. For the first issue of *Mersey Beat*, as he was calling it, Bill asked him to write a history of the Beatles' beginnings, and the result appeared on the front page. Entitled 'Being A Short Diversion On the Dubious Origins Of Beatles, Translated from the John Lennon', it would become one of the sacred Beatle texts, the canonical tale of the genesis of the Fab Four. It began: 'Once upon a time there were three little boys called John, George and Paul, by name christened. . . .' and went on to explain, among other things, where the group got its name: 'Many people ask what are Beatles? Ugh. Beatles, how did the name arrive? So we will tell you. It came in a vision – a man appeared on a flaming pie and said unto them "From this day on you are Beatles with an 'A'." Thank you, Mister Man, they said, thanking him.'[108] John's mock biblical chronicle is a classic offshoot of the British nonsense tradition, in which Lewis Carroll and the Goons are joined by Stanley Unwin, an English radio funnyman whose party piece was fluent conversational gobbledegookery. Unwin, who had been inspired by phrases like 'troutling streams' in James Joyce's *Finnegans Wake*, would later reappear to great effect in the pop world on the Small Faces' Tolkienish album 'Ogden's Nut-Gone Flake'. John's contribution, the first of several of his literary effusions to appear in the paper, was the opening salvo in Bill Harry's tireless campaign on behalf of his old friend's group.

Mersey Beat proved to be a great success, selling at least 5,000 copies from the start. The front page of the second number ran one of Astrid's photographs to illustrate the gripping news of the Beatles' recording with the hitmaking Kaempfert. Over 150 copies of the issue were ordered by the manager of the NEMS record shop near the Cavern, a failed RADA actor called Brian Epstein, so he was promptly invited to be a columnist as well. In August Epstein's record reviews would share a page with the Beatles' first published critical appreciation, a perceptive article by Bob Wooler. In the next issue Bob was rewarded by two of the many zany classified ads that John had taken to inserting in the paper: 'HEAR BOB WOOLER SING with the Beatles at Aintree Institute' and 'HEAR BOB BEATLES at the Woolerstute.'[109] Yet another Wooler article in October said that the Beatles were the top beat group in Liverpool, a judgement that would be endorsed in January when they won a readers' poll.

Bob would later say that other groups enviously called Bill Harry's paper 'The Mersey Beatle'.[110] In a way, that was the problem. If you discounted the beat colony in the stews of Hamburg, the Beatles' fame was showing no sign of ever spreading beyond Merseyside. In 1961, you had to be a success in London even to get a recording contract. From the perspective of the capital, everywhere else in Britain seemed hopelessly parochial, so it was rare for provincial groups to find even casual gigs there, and impossible to build up a following. There seemed to be no way out of this double bind.

As his 21st birthday approached, John wondered seriously about giving it all up. Ignoring any bookings they had, he dragged Paul to Paris for a fortnight to help him spend the huge gift of £100 sent by his aunt Mater in Scotland. There they met Jürgen Vollmer, who gave them both '*pilzkopf*' ('mushroom-head') haircuts as worn by Astrid and the others. In London on the way home they bought Chelsea boots (which would before too long be renamed as 'Beatle boots'.) After George had stopped laughing at them, they persuaded him to give up his hairgrease and brush his fringe forward as well.

Intrigued by all the interest in this new beat combo that he had been hearing and reading about, after Brian Epstein was asked in his shop to get a mysterious record by the Beatles called 'My Bonnie', he went to a lunchtime session at the Cavern, looking suave and dapper as always in his dark blue suit. He was embarrassed when Bob Wooler asked the crowd to give their 'rather famous' visitor a round of applause.[111] 'And there on a platform at the end on the cellar's middle tunnel stood the four boys,' Epstein would remember. 'Then I eased myself towards the stage, past rapt young faces and jiggling bodies and for the first time I saw the Beatles properly . . . There was some indefinable charm there. They were extremely amusing and in a rough "take it or leave" way very attractive.'[112] He spoke briefly to them afterwards, and would return several times to watch them again, wearing slightly less conspicuous clothes. He was bowled over by the experience. It was not merely their stage presence; there was something about the music too, though it wasn't normally his sort of thing. John later believed that this period would have been the best time to see the Beatles live: 'Our best work was never recorded . . . we were performers – in spite of what Mick [Jagger] says about us – in Liverpool, Hamburg and around the dance halls and what we generated was fantastic, where we played straight rock, and there was nobody to touch us in Britain. As soon as we made it, we made it, but the edges were knocked off.'[113]

Persistent rumours have suggested that the motive for Brian's initial interest in the Beatles was carnal. The sexual signals that they sent out were mixed. There was something strangely androgynous about 'the boys', as he would always like to think of them. Perhaps it was something to do with their strange, floppy haircuts, making them look, he thought, like the statue of Peter Pan in Sefton Park, or those boots. But willowy young men were not the sort of partners that Mr Epstein usually fancied. He tended towards tougher, more macho types, men who could hurt him if they wanted to (and sadly, in the course of a rather lonely gay life, they often did). There was one of those hard men in the Beatles, too, when you got to know them. That was John Lennon. 'There is,' Brian would write in 1964, 'in the set of his head a controlled aggression which demands respect.'[114] John was the one Brian watched most, and it wasn't only his head. His habitual stance on stage, with guitar high on his chest and feet far apart, threw into relief his leather-hugged eye-level crotch. 'I was very keen on splayed legs,'[115] Brian oddly remarks in his autobiography. In context, the phrase refers to fireside chairs, but it is

John, assertive and leather-clad in the Cavern

difficult not to read it as his subliminal admission of an
interest in John Lennon's provocative posture – or perhaps
a camp tease by Derek Taylor, the book's ghostwriter.

This is a contentious area in what is becoming known
as 'Beatles Studies': many commentators have speculated

along these lines, and just as many others have witheringly dismissed all speculation. Matters have not been clarified by John's various reported observations about his friendship with Brian Epstein and about homosexuality in general. These conflicting statements said to have been made by John range from Pete Shotton's 'And so I let him toss me off'[116] to Bill Harry's 'We didn't have an affair. But I liked playing it a bit faggy, you know, and all that – it was quite enjoyable.'[117] Paul McCartney said that John, asked if he had ever tried men, answered: 'No. I haven't met a fellow I fancy enough!'[118] Brian Epstein's true inner feeling for John Lennon is now an imponderable, as is John's behaviour with him when they were alone: it is surely sufficient to say that they had motives to spare and reasons aplenty to become part of each other's lives, and that John usually said yes to everything at first.

It may be more useful to suggest that Brian Epstein finally made the decision to manage the Beatles after he caught John in the Cavern singing 'Hello Little Girl', and discovered that he had written the number himself. They didn't often play their own songs: Bob Wooler once compiled a list of 93 different numbers that they had performed at the Cavern, of which only six were original compositions. Self-penned songs were still very rare in British beat groups, and the Beatles had as yet little confidence in their own writing abilities. To Brian, 'Hello Little Girl' was a sign of potential, and he would soon be urging them to write more. Within a few months, John and Paul would be claiming an entirely spurious back catalogue of over 100 Lennon-McCartney songs.

Brian invited the group to an initial meeting on 3 December. To provide weight, John brought along his greatest fan, Bob Wooler, and introduced him with the words: 'This is me Dad.'[119] Brian's publicity machine would soon be recycling passages from Bob's florid encomium to the group in the August *Mersey Beat*, such as the enticing 'Musically authoritative and physically magnificent, the Beatles are rhythmic revolutionaries with an act which is a succession of climaxes.'[120] Over the next few days Brian and John thrashed out what was by show business standards a very reasonable deal, giving the new manager one quarter of gross earnings, the remainder to be divided after expenses between the group, and on 24 January 1962 the Beatles finally signed the contract. By then Brian had already substantially increased their earnings by doubling the Cavern lunchtime fee from £5 to £10 for each appearance, and refusing to let them play anywhere else for less than £15.

Long before the paperwork was finished, once he had decided what he was going to do, Brian had worked fast. He invited John several times to his home to discuss the direction of the band. He also went round the Beatles's families, explaining what was happening. Mimi was wary at first, until he reassured her: 'I promise you, John will never suffer. He's the most important one.'[121] (She would later sum up Mr Epstein as 'a charming gentleman, a restless soul just like John.')[122] He had the group professionally photographed. By the second week of December he was already telling EMI that the Beatles 'play mostly their own compositions and one of the boys has written a song which I really believe to be the hottest material since "Living Doll".'[123] With the help of a rough tape he had made of a Cavern session, he managed to set up an audition in London with a record company, Decca. Organizing this from Liverpool had been far from easy: the Beatles' new manager was realizing that he needed to work twice as hard as any London counterpart would have done.

Brian informed the group that if they really wanted to succeed they had to build an image that was as far away from the Toxteth Teds as they could get. It was essential that they curb the wilder sides of their act. For the first time in his life John, infected by Brian's optimism, was prepared, very reluctantly, to accept unwelcome advice and direction. 'So it got to be Epstein saying, "Look, if you wear a suit, you'll get this much money . . ." Yeah man, all right, I'll wear a suit – I'll wear a bloody balloon if someone's going to pay me; I'm not in love with leather that much.'[124] The Beatles were told to give up smoking Woodbines in favour of the more

Tamed and groomed by Brian Epstein. The Beatles as they would soon become, with Ringo Starr

toney Senior Service, and not to smoke anything at all on stage, where they should also desist from eating, drinking, chewing gum, swearing or sleeping. They should jettison their jeans, stamp out their sneakers and lose their leather gear. They should work out a well-rehearsed set of songs, turn up to gigs in good time, perform for no more than an hour, and bow low to the audience when it was over. (John afterwards used to bow ridiculously low: a silent protest that became a habit.) 'We were in a daydream till he came along. We had no idea what we were doing. Seeing our marching orders on paper made it all look official . . . There were great fights between him and me, over me not wanting to dress up and he and Paul wanting me to dress up.'[125]

By March Brian had got them into grey lounge suits with narrow lapels. The suits would all soon fall to bits, unpicked by Cavern sweat, but the principle had been won. As the years went by, John Lennon would find it increasingly difficult to forgive himself for his capitulation to Brian's orthodoxy at this time, but he did not forget that without it, success might never have come.

The Decca audition, which took place on New Year's Day 1962, was disappointing for all of them, and particularly for John. They were nervous, and on Brian's advice had played a particularly anodyne selection of songs, with Paul in embarrassingly histrionic voice singing seven of the 15 numbers (including the charmless 'Besame Mucho', a song borrowed from the Coasters and seemingly dragged out on every possible occasion). John sang lead on only four, his own trusty 'Hello Little Girl', a lacklustre cover of Chuck Berry's 'Memphis', a reasonable version of 'Money (That's What I Want)' and an attempt at Phil Spector's debut single when he was in the Teddy Bears, 'To Know Her Is To Love Her' (which in 1973 John was to rerecord for Spector himself). Decca turned them down a month later.

Now armed with the professionally recorded Decca audition songs, as well as 'My Bonnie', which he had persuaded Polydor to release in the UK with the word 'Beatles' on the sleeve, Epstein redoubled his efforts in London. Though he managed to get the group a radio spot in front of a live audience on the BBC Light Programme's 'Teenager's Turn' in March – their first performance in suits – by May he was very despondent. With dwindling optimism, he approached a small label called Parlophone, part of the EMI group (which had already rejected the Beatles once, saying that they 'sounded like a bad recording of the Shadows.')[126] Parlophone was known as the company's 'joke' label: with only one Top Ten entry in six years – for the Temperance Seven – it issued mostly glum Scottish acts, jolly novelty songs and spoken word comedy records. The Goons were on its books, but Charlie Drake was too.

Accordingly, Parlophone's Artists and Repertoire man, George Martin, was desperate for something new. When he heard the Decca tape he was struck by 'an unusual quality of sound, a certain roughness that I hadn't encountered before.'[127] It was unusual for beat groups to have three capable lead singers, and to be able to cope so well harmonically. He offered them a recording test. This was not a firm contract, since it was subject to Martin's final approval, but Brian, who was unfamiliar with the term, was ecstatic. Thinking it meant that he had made a definite deal, he wired the boys at once and told them to rehearse new material. John's postcard back read: 'When are we going to be millionaires?'[128]

John and the others were away on what was being billed as their European Tour. In fact the Beatles were making their third visit to Hamburg, at a new venue, the Star-Club, for which Brian had managed to get them the unprecedented sum of £180 a week. It had been the first time any of them had ever flown, and they were in high spirits when they touched down, since Gene Vincent was also going to be on the bill at the club. Maybe they would play together. Astrid was waiting for them at the airport, and she had something terrible to tell them. Stuart was dead. He had died the day before, with her in an ambulance, on the way to the hospital.

It had been a brain haemorrhage. Yes, there had been warnings, temper tantrums, terrible headaches and temporary bouts of blindness: nobody had known what to do. On Stuart's last visit to Liverpool in February to introduce Astrid to his family, he had looked ill, pale as a ghost and thin, but John hadn't particularly noticed. Wanting him back in Liverpool, John had even got Brian to hint of a job for him in some artistic capacity with NEMS, though he hadn't risen to the bait. By the time

81

Stuart Sutcliffe

that Stuart's worried mother had found him a specialist, he was back in Hamburg with Astrid.

Looking back, of course, it seemed obvious that something serious had been wrong with him for some time. His handwriting had gone to hell, for one thing, and *Spotlight on Johnny*, a novel he had been trying to write about himself and John, had ground to a halt. John had kept up their friendship by post. In his letters he put, as he told Stuart, 'a little part of my almost secret self in the hands of someone miles away who will wonder what the hell is going on or just toss it off as toilet paper.'[129] Replying in ever more frantic tones, Stuart adopted the role of Jesus Christ, and John played along as his John the Baptist. For both of them, the rather gloomy correspondence had been a way of defining themselves, weighing up who they were in the scheme of things, more an act of meditation than one of communication. But it had kept their special friendship alive.

John's reaction to the loss would be observed in different ways by those around him. He refused to talk to anyone about Stuart, but over the next seven weeks in Hamburg, almost anything he did would be ascribed to delayed shock. There are descriptions of him wandering the Reeperbahn in his underpants, and being beaten up after smashing a bottle over somebody's head. When Brian Epstein came out to see how the boys were getting on, John had a one-sided shouting match with him at the end of a boozy evening, and drenched him in beer. He was kind but firm with Astrid, however, and managed to coax her out to the club sometimes, and he was gentle with her mother, taking her comfortably in his arms. However, perhaps the simplest and best assessment of what Stuart had meant to John was Mimi's: she called Stuart Sutcliffe 'the only real friend John ever had.'[130] The group got back from Hamburg with another Polydor recording session (more rejuvenated oldies with Tony Sheridan) under their belts. Then, on June 6, it was straight into the studio to meet George Martin, and to play him some of the 'new material' that Brian had requested in his telegram, including McCartney's 'Love Me Do' and 'PS I Love You', and Lennon's 'Ask Me Why'. It did the trick, for Martin not only liked what he heard, he liked the Beatles too (though George Harrison, famously, did not like his tie). There was much relief on all sides when he confirmed that he would indeed be signing the contract to the Beatles' first record deal. The starting pistol had been primed, and it was about to go off.

83

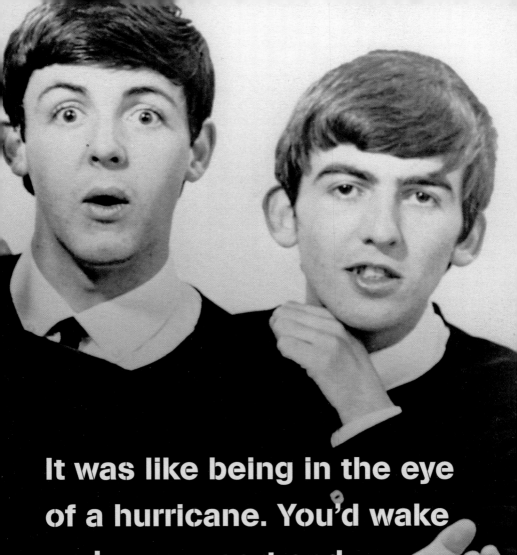

It was like being in the eye of a hurricane. You'd wake up in a concert and think, 'Wow, how did I get here'[131]

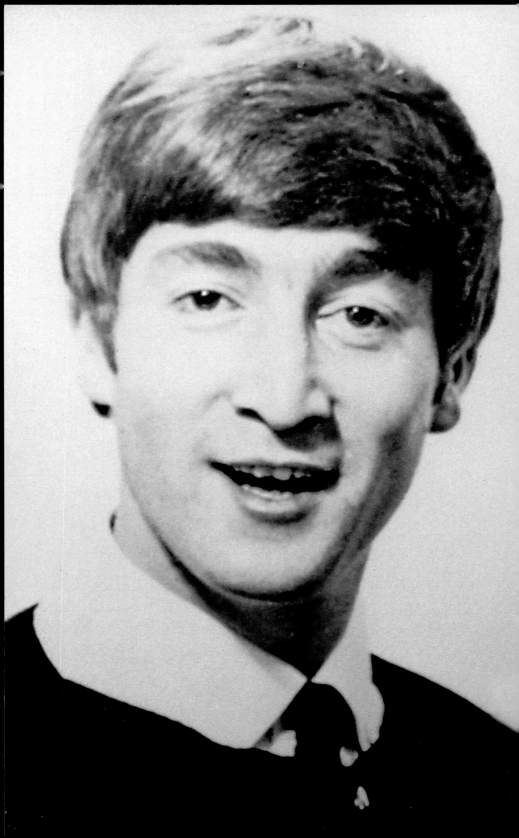

Grinning at Nothings

Bob Wooler's 'Welcome Home Beatles' show at the Cavern on 9 June 1962 broke all records, packing 900 fans into a venue usually called full at 500. At the beginning of July, with their new friend, Gene Vincent, they played the old Hamburg standby, 'What'd I Say'. Various recordings of the Beatles were made in the Cavern at this time, including this one, but few have ever seen the light of day. The acoustics were difficult. After George Martin saw the Beatles in action there, he proposed recording a live album, but concluded that the echo made it impossible.

To separate his Beatle activities from the family business, which was still dominated by his father, Brian set up NEMS Enterprises, putting Peter Brown – another 'RADA flouncer', according to Bob Wooler[132] – in charge of the record shops. Brown would soon enough be sucked into the Beatles' support team too. The Parlophone contract was finally signed and sealed in July. The group was offered one penny per £1 on record sales, rising annually for four years by one quarter of a penny. If John did his sums (which he probably didn't), he could have worked out that every time the Beatles sold £100 worth of records, he would get just over one shilling and sixpence, enough to buy three scotch and cokes, and that would be before tax. At this rate, it would be a while before he became a millionaire.

But while records did not pay well, chart success was all-important. A hit would allow the group to charge higher prices for their live performances, one way in which real money could be made. Even with nothing more than the prospect of a recording deal to boast about, Brian was already proving very successful at finding worthwhile dates and negotiating good appearance fees. Before the end of June, in a pattern that would be repeated, the Beatles appeared second on the bill to Bruce Channel, then touring Britain to capitalize on his recent big hit, 'Hey Baby'. Not only would the song join the Beatles' repertoire for a time, but John would filch the distinctive wailing sound of Channel's harmonica player, Delbert McLinton, to use in 'Love Me Do'.

Before John recorded his now familiar descending intro to that song, which would become the Beatles' first single, there was something important to take care of. At the Parlophone 'recording test' in June, George Martin had intimated to Brian that he was not particularly impressed by Pete Best's drumming. This might have been of no great consequence: temporary studio drummers were often used to ensure that the tempo at the end of a track matched that at the beginning. However, Paul and George had been muttering about Pete behind his back for months, and Martin's criticism was the trigger they needed. After discussing it with John, they all decided that Pete should be asked to leave the group.

They already had a perfect replacement. Ringo Starr, since their first friendship in Hamburg, had often said how much he would like to join the group. 'Ringo was a star in his own right in Liverpool before we even met,' John Lennon said later. 'Whatever that spark is in Ringo, we all know it, but we can't put our finger on it. . . . There's something in him that is projectable.'[133] So Ringo was phoned at Skegness, where he was appearing at Butlin's, and he agreed to start in a few days. Brian was left with the unpleasant job of breaking the news to Pete, who was shocked to the core. He refused to appear for his last gigs before Ringo took over, and was never to speak to any of the Beatles again. 'We were cowards when we sacked him,' said John. 'We made Brian do it. But if we'd told him to his face, that would have been much nastier. It would probably have ended in a fight.'[134]

Brian put pressure on Bill Harry to report in *Mersey Beat* that the change of drummers had been amicable, but there was pandemonium among Pete's many female admirers, who accused the other Beatles of being jealous of his saturnine, James Dean looks. George was caught in a mêlée of protest and given a black eye, and Brian avoided the Cavern for days, and then appeared with a bodyguard. But Ringo, with his indefinable charm, would soon be accepted as an essential member of the Beatles. It helped that, unlike Pete Best, he was happy to shave his 'sidies' and submit to the regulation moptop. John summed it up: 'Pete Best is a good drummer; Ringo is a good Beatle.'[135]

In August, Cynthia nervously broke the news to John that she was pregnant. 'I watched his face drain of all its colour, and fear and panic creep into his eyes,'[136] she would recall. After the initial shock, John said that they must of course get married. It was the only thing to do in those days, short of a career-wrecking scandal: 'I got married before I even knew what religion my wife was, I never asked her.'[137] Mimi had never much warmed to Cynthia. When she heard the news she was livid, and the night before the wedding caused a terrible scene in Mendips, which ended (in Mimi's version, at least) with John almost in tears, moaning 'I don't want to get married'.[138] On 23 August the wedding went ahead without Mimi at the Mount Pleasant Registry Office – where, 24 years before, Freddie Lennon had married Julia Stanley in a ceremony that was as cursory as this one.

It was not a very romantic occasion. Paul was John's best man, but the only others present were George Harrison, Brian Epstein and Cynthia's brother Tony and his wife. During the ceremony they were all convulsed with mirth by the sound of a pneumatic drill outside. 'It was all a laugh,' John would say. 'I couldn't hear a word the bloke was saying. Then we went across the road and had a chicken dinner.'[139] Brian's wedding present to the couple was almost the only one they got, and though it didn't cost him anything, it was a generous one: John and Cynthia were invited to live, rent-free, in the flat near the Art College which he had previously reserved for his own obscure encounters. That evening John was back again with the boys, on stage in Chester.

In December, Cynthia, already feeling nervous and tense in Brian's flat while John was away on gigs almost every night, was persuaded after problems with the pregnancy to move in to Mendips, but that didn't work very well either. After the baby was born Mimi grew even bossier, and by early summer Cynthia would have moved again into a cheap Liverpool bedsit. ('Two women loving the same man . . . an impossible situation,' is how she would read it later.)[140] Meanwhile, the marriage was not mentioned to the press, and for weeks John even kept it a secret from Ringo: 'I did feel embarrassed about it though, you know, walking about married. It was like walking about with odd socks on or your flies open.'[141]

On 5 October 1962, 'Love Me Do' was released as the Beatles' first single on the Parlophone label, and published by the London music publisher Dick James. It had a simple, rough 'bluesy' feel. Written by Paul with help from John, the song was lyrically bare to the point of vapidity, and its directness, crudity even, was striking – this was a period when most beat groups looking for chart success were issuing perky, well-crafted ditties, laden with the usual amorous clichés. The song had not been George Martin's first choice, but the Beatles had insisted that his candidate single, a bouncy off-the-peg tune called 'How Do You Do It?', would damage their credibility as rockers. On the B side of the record, by contrast, was the more melodic 'P S I Love You', a soft romantic ballad by Paul that was popular with the Beatlettes. 'They're buying our record,' John crowed, 'real people are buying our fucking record!'[142] Brian Epstein certainly was: as a Liverpool record retailer he was in a position to buy (and also, of course, to sell) quite large numbers of the disc. Whether it was thanks to NEMS overordering or not, by December 'Love Me Do' had made it to No 17.

From previous contracts the group had two final

John playing in the Cavern on the return visit of 1963

fortnights to fulfil in Hamburg before the end of the year.
Both took place at the Star-Club. John naturally seized
the opportunity of going wild before he got back under
Epstein's thumb, and some of his merriment was captured
on an unofficial tape of one of the Beatles' Hamburg
performances. The tape was later discovered in Liverpool
and issued as a double album in 1977 as 'The Beatles Live!
At the Star-Club in Hamburg, Germany; 1962'. Though the
sound quality is dire and the Beatles are clearly not trying

very hard, it is the only recording that really captures any of the atmosphere of the group's German apprenticeship.

On the second of the two German visits the Beatles shared the bill with their old idol Little Richard. They sat in awe backstage as he read them passages from the Bible – though by the end of the fortnight John had reverted to form and was calling him 'Grandad' and telling him to shut up.[143] The legendary R&B singer said, inexplicably to today's ears: 'Man, those Beatles are fabulous! If I hadn't seen them I'd never have dreamed they were white. They have a real authentic negro sound.'[144] Little Richard's campily extravagant statement was an augury of things to come: during the rest of the 1960s, as the Beatles became (as Brian kept saying they would) 'bigger than Elvis', they would be gathered up in a whirlwind of exaggerated superlatives, hyped press statements, rumours and inventions. For John Lennon in particular, normal reality would be suspended: it would be possible to argue that it was never to return

The Beatles' second single, 'Please Please Me', was what really broke the group through the sound barrier. John's joyous anthem was a more complex and sophisticated piece of music than 'Love Me Do', and was far more exciting as well. 'It was my attempt at writing a Roy Orbison song, would you believe it?', John would comment in 1980. 'I wrote it in the bedroom in my house at Menlove Avenue, which was my auntie's place . . . I remember the day and the pink coverlet on the bed and I heard Roy Orbison doing "Only The Lonely" or something . . . And also I was always intrigued by the words of [sings] "Please lend your little ears to my pleas" – a Bing Crosby song. I was always intrigued by the double use of the word "please". So it was a combination of Bing Crosby and Roy Orbison.'[145] The song had failed to take light until George Martin suggested boosting the tempo. He had also recommended adding a harmonica intro like that on 'Love Me Do', to act as a recognition factor for the group – and he would insist on it again for their third single, 'From Me To You'. Martin's continued contribution to the music of the Beatles is hard to overestimate: they were extremely receptive and quick to learn, and he taught them a great deal. However, they also constantly surprised him with unexpected rhythmic, melodic and harmonic ideas, ideas that frequently ran counter to Tin Pan Alley orthodoxy – the last thing that anyone expected from a musically illiterate guitar group from the sticks.

In the second week of 1963, 'Please Please Me' was released, with John's 'Ask Me Why' on the flipside. It began chugging up the charts, and by the end of February had become the Beatles' first number one in almost all the UK charts. Though at first George Martin had little faith in the Lennon-McCartney songbook, after their second single he was happy to assist the group on an LP, also to be called 'Please Please Me', which would contain a majority of their own songs. Martin wanted to recreate as far as possible the spontaneity that he had observed in the Cavern, so, apart from the four songs that had already been released on the singles, the whole album was recorded in a day. It opened with 'I Saw Her Standing There', a rock 'n' roll original mostly by Paul that often used to kick off their Cavern set, but the most memorable performance was the last one to be recorded, a wild cover version of the Isley Brothers' 'Twist And Shout', performed by a shirtless John whose throat had finally succumbed to a bad cold: 'I couldn't sing the damn thing. I was just screaming. My voice wasn't the same for a long time after. Every time I swallowed, it was like sandpaper.'[146] Though the album had its quota of duds, 'Twist And Shout' in particular gave it an edge that proved that the Beatles could transfer their rocker credentials to disc in spite of the civilizing influences of Brian Epstein and George Martin.

'Please Please Me' got to number one in the album charts on 8 May. It would remain there for 30 weeks, still a British record. In 1963, their next three singles, 'From Me To You', 'She Loves You' and 'I Want To Hold Your Hand', were also to reach the top. They were all more or less 50-50 collaborations between John and Paul, written in hotel rooms or on the bus between gigs. Though for years people assumed that this pattern continued, in fact the majority of Lennon-McCartney songs would in the future be written solo, and then beaten into shape by the whole group in the studio, under the eye of George Martin. The pair composed quite distinctive sorts of tune. To put it at its simplest, Paul tended to send his melodies swooping dramatically up and down the octave and beyond, with the words perhaps something of a secondary consideration, while John was more likely to make verses whose tune sidled around the chord, appearing to emerge out of the lyric like a form of emphatic speech. (Extreme examples of the contrast might be Paul's 'When I'm Sixty-four' and John's 'Lucy In The Sky With Diamonds', both on 'Sgt Pepper's Lonely Hearts Club Band'.) There would naturally be many exceptions to the pattern, and since their styles complemented each other well, sometimes, particularly in the early years, John would add a 'middle eight' to a song of Paul's or vice versa. A good rule of thumb for establishing which of the Beatles was the primary composer of which song is to identify who was the lead singer, since each usually sang his own.

The year was a frenzy of activity. They took on as a second roadie the 'gentle giant', Mal Evans, a telephone installer whom they had found in the Cavern. The Beatles' first nationwide television broadcast, on 19 January, was followed by many more. On radio they gave frequent interviews, developing a engaging style of inconsequential banter that allowed John, for one, to insult anyone he liked without causing offence. Over the next two years they would record literally hundreds of songs, old and new, for BBC broadcast – the Light Programme even ran a 15-part series called *Pop Go the Beatles*. At the same time they were embarking on their first tours of real theatres around the country: 'Touring was a relief, just to get out of Liverpool and break new ground. We were beginning to feel stale and cramped.'[147] They began in February at the bottom of the bill to the 16-year-old British singing sensation, Helen Shapiro, who rather fell for John. By the early summer they were the headlined closing act on a shared tour with the great Roy Orbison. There were summer residencies by the seaside, which usually meant two concerts a day for a week or so, in Margate, Weston-Super-Mare, the Channel Islands, Llandudno, Bournemouth and Southport. In the autumn there would even be a short foreign tour, in Sweden.

As their audiences grew, John and Paul worked hard on stage technique. John thought he 'might lie on the floor like Al Jolson' (as Freddie Lennon must have done in his perfomances), but instead he practised what they called 'grinning at nothings'.[148] By late spring the screaming had begun. They discovered that when they shook their heads while singing the falsetto 'oooohs' that punctuate their early songs, the screams doubled in volume.

All this new celebrity demanded of the group a high degree of discipline and a willingness to take orders under conditions of great stress. They were expected to appear happy, cheerful and charming at all times. For John Lennon, this was asking the impossible. On 12 March, claiming a 'heavy cold', he left the others to perform without him in Bedford, and that night, rather than going home to be nursed by Cynthia, he went drinking in a Liverpool club until after four in the morning, before rejoining the others three days later. As the Beatle phenomenon grew, so did Brian Epstein's power over the press, which was avid to be given any titbit about the group, and he was usually able to cover up any occasions when John went off the rails.

At six in the morning on 8 April 1963 Cynthia gave birth to a boy in the same Liverpool hospital where Julia Lennon had been declared dead less than five years before. The baby would be called Julian in memory of the grandmother he was never to meet. The night before, John had been performing on the south coast, and he was due in London the day after: so it was nearly a week before his schedule brought him north again and he could briefly visit the hospital (in disguise) to see his wife and child. All accounts state how delighted he seemed. The birth, like the wedding, was kept out of the press.

A few days later, Brian allowed his 'boys' a holiday. He invited John to come alone to Spain with him, and rather

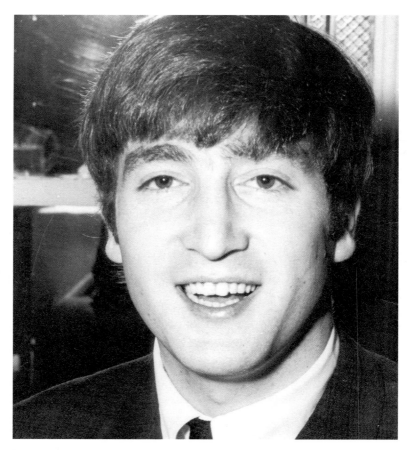

John caught smiling in a publicity shot

to everyone's surprise, he went. This holiday, and its violent aftermath, is a murky episode in John Lennon's biography, which once again is linked to Epstein's homosexuality. For of course, people in Liverpool gossiped. 'It started off all the rumours that he and I were having a love affair, but not quite – it was never consummated,' John later recalled. 'But we did have a pretty intense relationship . . . I was pretty close to him because if somebody's going to manage me, I want to know them inside out. And there was a period when he told me he was a fag and all that. It was my first experience with someone I knew was homosexual. We used to sit in cafés and Brian would look at all the boys and I would ask,

96

"Do you like that one? What about this one?"'[149]

In June, after they got back, Paul had a party for his 21st birthday. By most accounts, Bob Wooler, who was a guest, made a suggestive quip to John about his 'honeymoon' with Brian in Spain. John went berserk, beating him up badly in front of everyone: 'He called me a queer so I battered his bloody ribs in.'[150] Bob, who late in life would grudgingly admit that he himself was gay, never afterwards spoke precisely of what was behind the assault: 'Only Brian Epstein, John Lennon and myself know what happened,' he would say, 'if you get me a deal for £20,000 . . . I will change my mind.'[151] No deal was ever made.

Whatever triggered John's attack, it has never been in doubt that during these years he was primarily an active and predatory heterosexual. John would pick up and ravish as many women as he could, new ones if possible, and opportunities were many: the contraceptive pill, available in the UK since 1961, allowed starchasing to become almost a sport for certain female fans. Though some have suggested he was also playing some sort of sexual double game to control Epstein, no credible evidence has ever come to light. Indeed, many have felt that his constant rather cruel teasing of Epstein for being a *Queer Jew* (which John would suggest he call his autobiography) rather proved the opposite, though once again, it does nothing of the sort. John later tried to rationalize: 'I must have had a fear that maybe I was homosexual to attack him like that and it's very complicated reasoning. But I was very drunk and I hit him and I could have really killed somebody then. And that scared me.'[152] All Brian's influence failed to keep this incident out of the papers: the story appeared in the *Daily Mail*, – and it would in fact be the Beatles' first piece of national coverage.

Some six weeks later, Bob Wooler gave the Beatles his usual warm welcome to the Cavern stage. It would be the last time they were ever to appear there: the Cavern could no longer cover Brian's fee, as he had put it up to £300. Bob gave no hint of what John Lennon had done to him: he had been given £200 in exchange for his silence.

It's not everyone what has a real cripple for a father[153]

Working Like a Dog[154]

And then John Lennon and the Beatles were gone from Liverpool, and their centre of operations moved to London. 'That was a great period,' John said. 'We were like kings of the jungle then, and we were very close to the Stones.'[155] Mick Jagger would remember the Beatles coming like a 'four-headed monster'[156] into Crawdaddy's in Richmond to see them play. John and Paul gave them a song, 'I Wanna Be Your Man', which became their first single. While the newspapers reported fierce rivalry between the two groups, it wasn't quite so in reality: John envied the Rolling Stones' refusal to compromise with respectability (which of course was part of their appeal), but he knew, like everyone else, that in terms of popularity the Beatles were way off the scale. By the time that 'She Loves You' came out in August, with its trademark 'Yeah, Yeah, Yeah', it was evident that the Beatles phenomenon was something unique.

The old guard was sniffy at first: Edward Heath, a leading Conservative politician, complained that their language was 'unrecognizable as the Queen's English';[157] when John was asked about this in a TV interview he put on a toffee-nosed voice and began a flippant reply, but then he suddenly stopped, looked straight into camera and said seriously: 'We're not going to vote for Ted.'[158] His Liverpool accent was a considered stance, as he would state in another, later, televised interview: 'We were the first working-class singers that stayed working-class and didn't try to change our accents – which in England were looked down upon and probably still are.'[159] John's self-conscious identification with the working class (of which he was hardly a member) was part of a nationwide swing against the old Conservative/conservative consensus. In 1963 the Profumo scandal had mortally wounded Harold Macmillan's government. A year later, after much ridicule in the new satirical media (the magazine *Private Eye* and BBC television's *That Was The Week That Was* in particular) the old élite would be ousted by Harold Wilson's Labour Party, which claimed to offer the 'white heat' of technology in place of what was now perceived as the Tories' class-ridden paternalism. By then Wilson would have hoisted himself onto the Beatles bandwagon by presenting them with the 'Show Business Personality of the Year' awards for 1963 – John thanked him for the 'purple hearts'.[160]

'The people in the cheaper seats clap your hands, and the rest of you if you'd just rattle your jewellery.' John would make his most famous remark of all in front of the Queen Mother at the Royal Command Performance on 4 October 1963. 'I was fantastically nervous, but I wanted to say something to rebel a bit, and that was the best I could do.'[161] His well planned witticism was delivered with exactly the right level of winsome cheek, but John's embarrassment was palpable. Before the show he had apparently tortured Brian by saying that he was going to ask the toffs to rattle their 'fucking' jewellery. The Command Performance was a one-off: for John it was a grovel too far; though the Queen Mother had found the Beatles 'most intriguing'[162] and they were invited back several times, they never again accepted.

Brian was convinced that whatever worries John might give him, fate had delivered someone remarkable into his hands. In his 1964 autobiography he would describe him in terms that left his opinion in no doubt: 'John Lennon, . . . the dominant figure in a group which

In the lineup after the Royal Command Performance

is, virtually, without a leader, is in my opinion, a most exceptional man. Had there been no Beatles and no Epstein participation, John would have emerged from the mass of the population as a man to reckon with. He may not have been a singer or a guitarist, a writer or a painter, but he would have certainly have been a Something. You cannot contain a talent like this.'[163] Beatles fans were no less enthusiastic. Hysterical crowds met them wherever they went. Sometimes the group had to be protected from the fans by steel mesh in front of the stage: 'if they press any harder, they'll come through as chips,'[164] commented John. In Dublin for their only concert in the Republic, Donal McCann, then a young reporter, asked him if he believed in God. John's reply, 'I have certain reservations,' was considered unprintable by McCann's 'strong Catholic evening paper'.[165] The Irish fans laid on 'the biggest riot yet',[166] with cars overturned and shop windows broken, and John hardly glimpsed the city of his ancestors. The mayhem was observed by the Liverpudlian writer Alun Owen, who was preparing a screenplay for their first film, tentatively entitled 'Beatlemania.'

The media were by this time giving the 'Beatles effect' widespread coverage. The heavyweight newspapers now mentioned the group almost as often as the tabloids did, examining the phenomenon from all directions: the Beatles were dragged as a cultural indicator into discussions of hundreds of quite unrelated subjects. Even the *New York Times* devoted three pages to the British Beatle frenzy in December. Analogies were drawn between Beatlemania and the mass hysteria seen in pre-war Germany. The *Daily Telegraph* spoke on 2 November of Hitler's Nuremberg rallies, but Ringo simply enlisted the fans for the Allied cause, quipping 'I reckon if we'd used this lot in the war, we'd have overrun Germany in about a fortnight.'[167] When a psychiatrist made the comparison John said he was obviously out of his mind himself.[168]

The Beatles' second album, 'With The Beatles', was released in the UK on 22 November 1963, the day that President Kennedy was assassinated in Dallas. The blanket news blitz from America that followed had no measurable effect on the album's fortunes, however: it at last toppled 'Please Please Me' from the number one spot in the charts two weeks later, and would remain there for almost five months. Refreshingly, the Beatles were not shown smiling on the sleeve (which used an arty photograph inspired by Astrid Kirchnerr's heavily shadowed Hamburg shots), but their confidence shone through on the record: the fact that its first five songs were Lennon-McCartney originals was seen at the time as an extraordinary achievement. 'With The Beatles' was a better album than its predecessor: several tracks, such

Brian Epstein relaxing with 'the boys' in a Paris hotel after a concert

as John's cover versions of Berry Gordy's pre-Motown number, 'Money (That's What I Want)', or the Miracles' 'You Really Got A Hold On Me' – or indeed Paul's original, 'All My Loving' – would certainly have been hits if issued as singles. By now, however, the Beatles knew that they were producing enough good material for both singles and LPs. Particularly powerful album tracks could always be reissued on EPs ('extended play' 45s), which usually carried four tracks and had their own charts. It has been estimated that before 1964, John and Paul had performed over 300 known different songs on stage together.[169] With such a back catalogue, and since they were now writing more than ever before, as well as tackling cover versions of songs that had never been part of their live act, there was no reason to ask fans to buy anything twice.

On the strength of their work on this LP, serious music critics now began trying to analyse the appeal of the Lennon-McCartney songbook so far; in *The Times* William Mann ensured his immortality by writing of 'chains of pandiatonic clusters' and their use of the 'Aeolian cadence',[170] much to the amusement of John, who thought Aeolian cadences sounded like exotic birds. In *The Sunday Times* the critic Richard Buckle went even further two days later, calling them 'the greatest composers since Beethoven'.[171] Gradually, in John at least, the idea was taking hold that their music was indeed art, a judgement that quite soon he would take as self-evident.

The Beatles had devoted 1963 to subduing Britain; they spent 1964 taking over the rest of world. The campaign started modestly enough, with three weeks in the Olympia Theatre, Paris, where, in his spare time, John wrote several songs for the forthcoming film. And then, soon after the news came that 'I Want To Hold Your Hand' had reached number one in the USA, they were off in February for their first American trip.

The story of how the Beatles took America by storm after a record 73 million watched them on the Ed Sullivan Show is a familiar one. At the airport press conference, when John was asked whether he came from a showbiz family he replied, 'Well, me dad used to say me mother was a great performer.'[172] The remark set the tone for the dozens of irreverent radio interviews and press briefings that would follow, lapped up by a nation eager to forget JFK's death for a time. 'We were funny at press conferences because it was all a joke . . . It was just Fifth-Form humour, the sort you laugh at in school.'[173] But while John revelled in the triumph, a little of this sort of thing went a long way. At their two Carnegie Hall shows 'it was just a sort of circus where we were in cages. We were being pawed and talked at and met and touched, backstage and onstage. We were just like animals.'[174] There were more unpleasant moments at the British Embassy in Washington, where someone snipped off a lock of Ringo's hair: 'Suddenly, you're doing exactly what you don't want to do with people you can't stand, you know, people you hated when you were ten,' John recalled later. 'I walked out of that, swearing at all of them.'[175] In terms of coverage, of course, it was all worth it. During this first American visit, apart from the television spots, they played only three live sets in two venues, and the country wanted much more. By early April the Billboard Hot 100 was in a state never seen before or since: the Beatles occupied the top five places, and had about ten more singles further down. In the album chart they were fixtures at numbers one and two. (Several different companies had USA rights over Beatles songs, and they were all cashing in 'before the bubble burst'.)

Back in Britain, John was much in demand as an interviewee, particularly after his book, *In His Own Write*, was published at the end of March by the literary publisher, Jonathan Cape, and became an instant success. Not so very different from *The Daily Howl*, it was a slim volume consisting of prose squibs and verses written for John's own amusement at odd moments during tours, and supplemented with drawings and a few pieces reprinted from *Mersey Beat*. (Unforgivably, almost all his pre-Beatles writings had been lost by the paper after he handed them in for possible publication.) 'I suppose it was all manifestations of hidden cruelties,'[176] John would comment, accurately enough, but reviewers in all the best places treated *In His Own Write* warmly (though often slightly condescendingly). The young Tom Wolfe was particularly perceptive: 'He seems to take the general format for his stories, fables, playlets, poems and drawings from a British humorist named Spike Milligan. But the underlying bitterness of much of what Lennon writes about marriage and family life, for example, as well as his Joycean excursions into language fantasies, are

John and Cynthia Lennon, at last a couple in public at the Dorchester Hotel

something else altogether.'[177] The repeated mention by reviewers of Joyce (whom John had never read) prompted Lennon to buy *Finnegans Wake*, but though he admired it, he was finally defeated by its linguistic pyrotechnics and contented himself with becoming a subscriber to the *James Joyce Quarterly* instead.

Marriage and family life were not currently priorities for the 'intellectual Beatle', as John was now being called. There were misunderstandings and growing resentments on both sides. Cynthia had incurred his fury by having Julian christened without telling him. Though she had accompanied him to America, where journalists in the know had blackmailed them into being photographed together publicly for the first time, everyone noticed how detached they seemed as a couple. In the summer of 1964, they moved into Kenwood, a 27-room 'old man's house' in the prim suburb of Weybridge in Surrey, and while it was being totally remodelled over the next year, relations between them cooled further, though they tried to keep a generally fairly civil truce.

If the withering of John's love for his wife was one problem, quite another was the surprise reappearance of his father, on April Fool's Day 1964. At this stage John never went into details about his family background: in public he would only say 'I used to have an auntie. And I had a dad whom I couldn't quite find.'[178] It had been almost two decades since John's parents had parted, and Freddie Lennon's life had been hard in the meantime. In 1949, he had been sentenced to six months after smashing a window in Oxford Street, apparently because he wanted to dance with a shop mannequin that looked like his beloved Julia. On release he tried to contact John, but Mimi told him that if he didn't leave them alone she would inform the boy that his father was a jailbird. Being an ex-convict, Freddie was then rejected by the Merchant Navy, and so, having lost his profession, he became effectively a tramp, taking casual work in hotel kitchens and the like. As John would later comment, his father 'lived the life of a drunk and almost a Bowery bum.'[179]

Garbled accounts of how John Lennon's ne'er-do-well dad had deserted him and then disappeared had been appearing in the papers, and journalists were now beginning to track Freddie down. Before they wrote any more lies about him, he decided to try to set the record straight with his famous son and a meeting was arranged. It would last only about ten minutes. John was very wary of this odd and rather nervous little man, and Freddie had no chance to say very much. Though John told Pete Shotton afterwards that his father was 'good news, a real funny guy – a loony just like me,'[180] contact was not maintained: John just did not trust him. Mimi had done her work well. His suspicions seemed confirmed when Freddie, under continued pressure from reporters (and poverty), sold a story to the gossip magazine, *Tit-bits*. When Jonathan Cape received the manuscript of John's next book (*A Spaniard in the Works*), it would contain a long, very nasty and very funny ode, entitled 'Our Dad'. One of the less cruel verses went:

'You don't want me around,' he said,
'I'm old and crippled too.'
We didn't have the heart to say
'You're bloody right it's true.'[181]

The Beatles' first world tour took place in June 1964. It began in Denmark, and took in Holland, Hong Kong, New Zealand and Australia. John would later be unable to remember one city from another, or even one tour from another, as the routine was invariable – travelling half asleep, cheeky press conferences, luxury hotel rooms, screaming crowds, inaudible concerts, pills, drink and every night, a choice of willing girls. 'It was some kind of scene on the road. Satyricon!' John exclaimed. 'There's photographs of me grovelling about, crawling about Amsterdam on my knees, coming out of whorehouses, and people saying "Good morning, John."'[182] His behaviour improved markedly when Mimi arrived for the Australian leg of the tour, where the Beatles were given their most spectacular reception so far. In Adelaide more than a quarter of a million people clogged the streets.

Everywhere they went they were dogged by the

handicapped. John hated it. He was well aware of the irony: as *In His Own Write* revealed, his default form of humour had always been the mockery of abnormalities; now he felt he was being surreally pursued around the world by spastics and cretins. At Sydney airport a crippled little boy was thrown into the Beatles' moving open-topped lorry; when Paul threw him back to his mother she pronounced him cured. 'John was allergic to cripples,' George would remember. 'You can see in all our home movies, whenever you switch a camera on John, he goes into his interpretation of a spastic. It's not very nice to be afflicted, so John had this thing that he'd always joke about it. I think the reality was too much for him.'[183] On the American tour later in the year there would be even more of them.

The film they had shot in March and April had been renamed *A Hard Day's Night*, a phrase that John had already used in his book (though for some reason Ringo would always get the credit). In July both film and its accompanying LP came out to great acclaim. Alun Owen's screenplay was a modestly winning combination of fact and fiction, and gave the public its first clear view of the different personalities of each Beatle. 'Alun Owen only came with us for two days before he wrote the script,' John remarked later. 'We were a bit infuriated by the glibness of it. It was a good projection of one façade of us – on tour, in London and in Dublin . . . We *were* like that.'[184] Though the film had been shot in black and white on a low budget, everyone, even the critics, loved it. A comment in the *New York Herald Tribune* was typical: 'It really is an egghead picture, lightly scrambled, a triumph of the Beatles and the bald.'[185] John's screen performance was commended by the film's prematurely balding director Richard Lester; John told interviewers that after the Beatles had run their course in five years or so he might take up acting as a profession. He didn't, of course, but in 1966 Lester would give him the interesting supporting role of the kleptomaniac loner, Private

111

Gripweed, in his anti-war satire, *How I Won The War*.

If *A Hard Day's Night* achieved a surprising degree of excellence in the uninspiring genre of the musical bio-flick, it was more than matched by the album of the same name, on which ten of the 13 tracks were compositions of John's, many of them written to order and at speed. It became the fastest-selling album ever in the UK, selling over 1.5 million copies in two weeks. From what the late Ian MacDonald called 'the mighty opening chord of "A Hard Day's Night" (G eleventh suspended fourth)'[186] to the subdued fading promise of 'I'll Be Back', which ends side two, this was the first Beatles album that hung together as a coherent creation. The music was more complex than before – the title song used 13 chords, rather more than pop music's traditional three – and so were the words. 'I'll Cry Instead', for example, sounds like a bouncy rockabilly love song, but it is really an anatomy of the singer's anger and depression. Confident that his audience would not notice what his lyrics were actually saying, John begins with the words: 'I've got every reason on earth to be mad, 'Cos I've just lost the only girl I had. If I could get my way, I'd get myself locked up today, But I can't, so I'll cry instead.' As the song continues, in lines such as 'I've got a chip on my shoulder that's bigger than my feet',[187] John demonstrates a degree of self-analysis then almost unheard of in popular music. Until the end of his life, he would continue to use lyrics such as these to explore aspects of his often precarious mental state.

The quickfire, wisecracking Lennon of the film and the press conferences was indeed only one side of the story. John was currently coping with a crippling burden of pressures. An incomplete list of these might include the late nights, the travel and the jet lag, the lack of privacy, the demands of record companies and fans for regular, ever-improving creative product, the contrast between public adulation and private reality, the praise of sycophants, the constraints on behaviour imposed by Brian Epstein, the constant heavy drinking and the coarsening effect of breaking hearts all round the world. ('Never the same girl twice' was the unwritten law of touring.) When John got home, he had to cope with his own emotional tension and guilt, since Cynthia was clearly unhappy and Julian was failing to bond with his absent or preoccupied father. All these factors were damaging enough, but as John still kept his energy levels artificially high with amphetamines (now generally in the form of 'purple hearts'), the danger of complete paranoid breakdown was very real.

When the Beatles finally went on their first great tour of the USA at the end of the summer, stress fractures were already beginning to show. America was, if anything, even worse than Australia. Brian had hired football stadiums and convention halls for the concerts, the first ever held in such enormous venues, and they played to ecstatic audiences of 20,000 and more. They seemed to be surrounded by crazies. Female fans were seen throwing themselves to the ground to eat the grass that the Beatles had trodden on. There was a lively trade in canned 'Beatle breath', and fortunes were made by selling their bedsheets, cut up into tiny squares. John frequently tried to relieve some of his frustrations by shouting random insults and obscenities at audiences over the closing notes of the songs. In Indianapolis Ringo snapped, and went AWOL all one night. He appeared only just before the next concert, so strung out he could hardly walk. Luckily, even his drumming was inaudible over the non-stop screaming.

Earlier in the year, in Paris, the Beatles had discovered Bob Dylan for the first time, when they got hold of a copy of 'Freewheelin'', his 1963 album (which had both 'A Hard Rain's A-Gonna Fall' and 'Blowin' In The Wind' on it). 'We didn't stop playing it,' John remembered. 'We went potty on Dylan.'[188] On 28 August 1964, after their concert at Forest Hills, the singer was informed that he was welcome to visit their New York hotel. The encounter with Dylan that night would have far-reaching and unforeseen consequences, both for John personally and for his music.

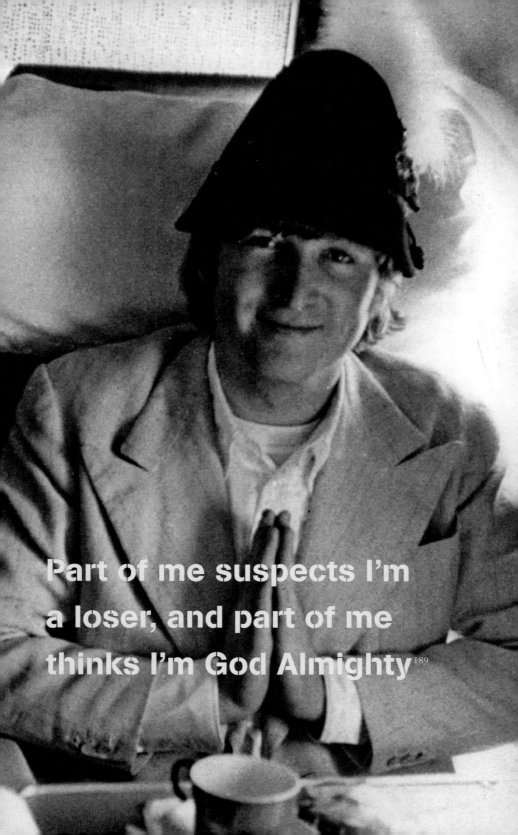

Part of me suspects I'm a loser, and part of me thinks I'm God Almighty[189]

Smoke and Mirrors

The story of Bob Dylan's visit to the Beatles' suite at the Delmonico Hotel that night is well known. When he suggested smoking some grass, he found it hard to believe that none of them were into it already. (John had tried pot before, but he had always been too drunk for the drug to work properly – the last time it had made him sick.) As there were cops outside, before lighting up they sealed under the door with towels. John was offered the joint first, and passed it dubiously to his 'royal taster', Ringo, who, unaware of the etiquette, went on tasting until it was all gone.[190] He then began to giggle infectiously, which set everyone else off, and so more 'jazz Woodbines' were rolled and in a short time they were all high as kites. 'We did nothing but laugh all night,' John remembered. '[Dylan] kept 'kept answering our phone, and saying, "This is Beatlemania here." It was ridiculous. He has got the same sense of humour as we have and our tastes in music, though not the same, cross somewhere.'[191]

The Beatles became enthusiastic potheads at once. 'We dropped drink, simple as that,' said John.[192] Their use of amphetamines also quickly died away. Cannabis reduced their stress levels, allowing them to relax at last, and the laughter it induced reinvigorated the bond between them. The effect of the drug on their music would not be clearly audible for some time. However, John

117

would insert the line 'Turn me on when I get lonely' into 'She's A Woman' (on the B side of their October single, 'I Feel Fine') as the first coded message to initiates that the Beatles were getting high.

'Beatles For Sale', their rather rushed fourth album, was released in December 1964 and shot to the top. 'The numbers on this LP are different from anything we've done before,' John announced, 'and you could call our new one a Beatles Country and Western LP.'[193] He had always liked the rather gloomy lyrics of country music, and Dylan had made it cool again. Nine of the 14 tracks featured John on lead vocals, and the album opened with two songs he had written earlier in the year, 'No Reply' and the introspective and Dylanesque 'I'm A Loser'. Short of new material, the Beatles filled out the album with vigorous cover versions from their old stage show, not all of which quite justified themselves. The increased sophistication of studio production helped, however, particularly the use of double tracking and echo – John, who unaccountably cringed at the sound of his own voice, was by now asking George Martin to change it electronically whenever possible: 'Smother it with tomato ketchup. Make it different.'[194]

In the spring the Beatles enjoyed themselves in the Bahamas and Austria making their second film with Dick Lester, then called *Eight Arms To Hold You*. Apart from the music, they had very little creative input in the film, 'partly,' as John admitted, 'because we were smoking marijuana for breakfast during that period. Nobody could communicate with us; it was all glazed eyes and giggling all the time.'[195] The drug was having a profound influence on John as a composer by now: when he was stoned it suddenly seemed important to express some of the insights that it gave him. His songs had sometimes been quite revealing, but usually more by accident than design. 'I wasn't too keen on lyrics in those days. I didn't think they counted.'[196] Now he remembered Bob Dylan saying, 'Hey, John, listen to the lyrics, man.'[197] When *A Spaniard In The Works*, his new book of pieces (written to

John drying his head after a swim in Miami

order, he said, out of a nightly bottle of Johnnie Walker),[198] was published in June, Dylan's point was reinforced by an interviewer who asked why he had never harnessed his literary imagination for his music.

But while cannabis was giving John and the other Beatles a lot of fun, another drug, so new that it was not even illegal, would soon have a far more radical effect on John Lennon and his work. During the second week of April 1965, John,

Cynthia, George and Patti Boyd, his girlfriend, were ritually given a sugar cube after a dinner party held by a dentist acquaintance. It was LSD. Ill prepared, all four were initially terrified by the optical illusions and mental delusions that ensued, and fled the dinner to take refuge, for some reason, in the new Pickwick Club. After more frightening experiences there and elsewhere around London, eventually they got back to George's house in Esher. Cynthia remembers: 'John was crying and banging his head against the wall.'[199] 'God, it was terrifying, but it was fantastic,' John exclaimed. 'George's house seemed to be just like a big submarine. I was driving it . . . I was pretty stunned for a month or two.'[200]

A couple of days later, when Dick Lester told him that the film was being renamed *Help!*, John took the cue and write the title song at once. Interestingly, he never acknowledged (or perhaps remembered) that 'Help!' was an acid song: 'When "Help" came out in '65, I was actually crying out for help. Most people think it's just a fast rock 'n' roll song. I didn't realise it at the time; I just wrote the song because I was commissioned to write it for the movie. But later, I knew I was really crying out for help. It was my fat Elvis period. You see the movie: he – I – is very fat, very insecure, and he's completely lost himself. And I am singing about when I was so much younger and all the rest, looking back at how easy it was.'[201]

Originally cast as a slower and more obviously thoughtful song than the final recording, the lyrics revealed in transparent code some of what John had uncovered about himself in the course of that first harrowing night, high on acid. ('When I was younger, so much younger than today, I never needed anybody's help in any way, But now these days are gone I'm not so self-assured, Now I find I've changed my mind, and opened up the doors . . . Help me get my feet back on the ground . . . My independence seems to vanish in the haze . . . I feel so insecure . . . I know that I just need you like I've never done before . . . Help me . . . Help me . . .'[202]) Though the doors of his perception had not been cleansed in the Huxleyan sense by his LSD experience, they had

120

been opened wide enough to allow him to catch frightening glimpses of himself in the drug's distorting mirror. (He had been reading Aldous Huxley: 'he's the new guvnor, it seems to me,' he had told Ray Coleman.)[203] John had made the first move in a dangerous process that would transform his life and work. At the beginning of 1966 he was to take the next step, using *The Psychedelic Experience*, Timothy Leary's loose adaptation of *The Tibetan Book of the Dead*, to embark on the systematic destruction of his ego according to the chemical guru's recommendations. Over the next two or three years, he would take LSD,[204] he claimed, over 1,000 times.

Help!, the film with its accompanying album, was released in July 1965. 'It was like having clowns in a movie about frogs,'[205] John would say. 'All the best stuff is on the cutting-room floor, with us breaking up and falling about all over the place, lying on the floor, incapable of saying a word.'[206] The group was touring much less now: there was a fortnight of concerts in Europe during a June heatwave, and in August another fortnight in the States, beginning at Shea Stadium, where John was seen (though not heard) playing the piano with his elbows to a world record audience of 56,000 fans. The Beatles were, he said, 'louder than God.'[207] On this trip they visited Elvis Presley, and John was disgusted to find that his old idol had sold out: 'It was like meeting Englebert Humperdinck.'[208] After John called President Johnson a warmonger, Elvis was apparently heard muttering, 'Someone ought to talk to the FBI about this sonovabitch.'[209] Brian Epstein would not be able to make John Lennon keep his political opinions to himself for much longer.

In October the Beatles collected their MBEs at Buckingham Palace – though Brian was ignored, and blamed establishment anti-Semitism. Aunt Mimi was with John at the ceremony, bursting with pride, and he gave her his medal to display in the new house he had bought for her by the sea in Dorset – Mendips had been under constant siege from fans. There were predictable protests from the Home Counties, which John later answered by saying: 'Lots of people who complained about us getting the MBE received theirs for

121

heroism in the war. Ours were civil awards. They got them for killing people. We deserve ours for not killing people.'[210] But what annoyed everyone most was when he pretended that the Beatles had smoked dope in Her Majesty's gents.

There would be a short swoop of concerts around Britain at the end of 1965, the group's final UK tour, as it turned out. From now on, apart from their ill-fated world tour in 1966, the Beatles would primarily be recording artists. 'Rubber Soul' came out in December, and in August 1966 'Revolver' (with a sleeve drawn by Klaus Voorman, who was now in London trying to make a name as a musician.) These albums would mark the transition of the Beatles' music from pop to rock. Their sense that they were in some sense frauds, interlopers in an alien musical tradition, was hinted at by the punning titles – 'soul' music, a refinement of R&B, was still largely a preserve of black musicians. (In 1969, John would use another joky title – 'Yer Blues' – to reflect similar uncertainty about his attempt at a 'proper' blues song.)

'"Rubber Soul" was the pot album, and "Revolver" was acid. I mean, we weren't all stoned making "Rubber Soul" because in those days we couldn't work on pot. We never recorded on acid, or anything like that. It's like saying, "Did Dylan Thomas write *Under Milk Wood* on beer?"'[211] Listening to 'Rubber Soul', most people did not identify the noisy intake of breath that punctuates John's 'Girl', a druggy fantasy of the arrival of his ever-elusive 'dream girl', as the sound of a joint being inhaled. However the song's floating, languid tone, and its questions about the validity of the work ethic, were unmistakable: 'Was she told when she was young that pain would lead to pleasure? Did she understand it when they said That a man must break his back to earn his day of leisure? Will she still believe it when he's dead?'[212] Equally, in 'Nowhere Man', 'Norwegian Wood' and most of all, the mantra-like 'The Word', John's lyrics were recognized for the first time to be conveying messages, if enigmatic ones – 'Say the word and you'll be free, Say the word and be like me, Say the word I'm thinking of, Have you heard, the word is love?'[213] The whole album looked forward to the coming of the love generation.

John's contributions to 'Revolver', however, told the world that something momentous had already happened. He summed it all up in three songs, 'She Said, She Said' (inspired by his second LSD trip), the equally psychedelic 'I'm Only Sleeping' and the extraordinary final track, 'Tomorrow Never Knows'. This was an unprecedented montage of many sound layers, accelerated sitar riffs, reversed guitar phrases on tape loops and alien cries and laughter, driven along by a solid, complex and almost oriental tattoo from Ringo, while miles away John's lazy voice, electronically enhanced to sound, he hoped, 'like the Dalai Lama and thousands of Tibetan monks chanting on a mountain top'[214], sang phrases derived from Timothy Leary: 'Turn on your mind, relax, and float downstream.'[215] Along with 'Rain', another of John's LSD-inspired compositions which appeared in June 1966 on the back of the single 'Paperback Writer', these songs testified that the Fab Four had changed beyond all recognition. 'Can you hear me that when it rains and shines, It's just a state of mind? Can you hear me? Can you hear me?'[216]

It was not that the revolution of the mid-1960s was caused by the Beatles, exactly. They were at once leaders and followers of what was happening in Britain. Beatles music formed the dominant soundtrack of a rapidly changing London, now the world centre of the 'Swinging Sixties'. This was more than a fashion trend writ large; it was the emergence of a whole alternative lifestyle, one that could coexist only awkwardly with the old authoritarian English way of life. The counterculture had spread from America in various ways, carried by dissident Americans who had fled to Britain to avoid the draft and were now denying the right of their parents' generation to tell them what to do. The city was suddenly a powerhouse of fun for the youth of the western world. Cultural disseminators such as Marc Boxer's *Sunday Times Magazine*, glossy periodicals like *Nova* and *Queen*, and even Richard Ingrams' *Private Eye* spread news of the 'youthquake' in London, with its sceptical attitude to authority and its visions of fresh openness, esoteric

Freddie Lennon the popstar

spirituality and sexual permissiveness. It was suddenly
obvious that all the old certainties could be questioned,
or even ignored. In 1965 Brian Epstein had with difficulty
managed to get the Beatles to keep their mouths shut about
politics, and particularly not to say anything in America
about the country's belligerent treatment of Vietnam. In

1966, John and George told him that they intended to sound off about anything they wanted.

Freddie Lennon was still being wooed by journalists anxious to make a fast buck out of him. At the beginning of the year, he was persuaded to record a song called 'That's My Life (My Love And Home)', which he had co-written as a sort of companion piece to John's recent nostalgic ballad, 'In My Life'. To the sound of the sea and a heavenly choir, Freddie, like another Ancient Mariner, told John and the British public the story of how, as he had 'sailed with the tides and lived on dreams', he had seen 'a lifetime in love go wrong'. 'I'll make no excuses for my own abuses,' he intoned in a voice uncannily like his son's, 'for life makes us all that way.'[217] It was an affecting performance, and after a week of radio play the single, issued on the Pye label, entered the charts at number 37. Brian Epstein (at John's prompting) then apparently let it be generally known that Freddie Lennon was not to be encouraged. All airplay ceased, and the record disappeared. Freddie appeared on John's doorstep soon afterwards to complain, but was told by John to fuck off.

The first quarter of 1966 was a time of rest for John. He spent most of it at home watching television. He was quoted as saying that TV was as good as pot – well, when you have been smoking pot, perhaps it is. Maureen Cleave's famous interview with John in his 'large, heavily panelled, heavily carpeted, mock Tudor house set on a hill' in Weybridge appeared in London's *Evening Standard* in March 1966. Though not a hostile portrait, the piece showed John at his most eccentric, and laziest: 'Sex is the only physical thing I can be bothered with any more.' He seemed disappointed that she did not ask him about Freddie, and spoke about him anyway: 'He was here a few weeks ago. It was only the second time in my life I'd seen him – I showed him the door. I wasn't having him in the house.' John seemed to be at a loose end. 'Weybridge won't do at all. I'll get my real house when I know what I want. You see, there's something else

I'm going to do, something I must do – only I don't know what it is. That's why I go round painting and taping and drawing and that, because it may be one of them. All I know is, this isn't it for me.'

The interview captured John on the cusp of change. From now on he would no longer be merely a member of the most successful pop group in the world, but also an unpredictable, outspoken public man with an often unpopular opinion on everything. He was currently reading extensively about religion, he told Cleave. 'Christianity will go. It will vanish and shrink. I needn't argue about that; I'm right and I will be proved right. We're more popular than Jesus now; I don't know which will go first – rock 'n' roll or Christianity. Jesus was all right but his disciples were thick and ordinary. It's them twisting it that ruins it for me.'[218] Though the article was enjoyed and forgotten in London, when John's remarks were republished in a teenage magazine in America a few months later and then broadcast on an Alabama radio station, a storm would break out in the USA. 'When I heard all the fuss,' John remarked later, 'I couldn't remember saying it.'[219]

In *Skywriting by Word of Mouth*, his posthumous collection of writings, John would comment: 'I always remember to thank Jesus for the end of my touring days; if I hadn't said that the Beatles were "bigger than Jesus" and upset the very Christian Ku Klux Klan, well, Lord, I might still be up there with all the other performing fleas! God bless America. Thank you Jesus.'[220] Not only the Klansmen objected: many radio stations refused to play Beatle music and thousands of good God-fearing middle Americans threw their records onto bonfires. On a final sour burst of touring, in July and August, the Beatles played as usual to audiences who were not listening – and when they did listen, as in Japan, it was embarrassing, because the group hadn't bothered to rehearse. In Japan too, there were death threats, apparently for desecrating the Nippon Budokan Hall; in the Philippines they narrowly escaped incarceration and injury after inadvertently snubbing Imelda Marcos, the President's wife.

An unhappy John immediately after publicly apologising to America.

When the Beatles reached America, terrified that they would be shot at during a concert, John had to apologise on live TV for his casual remarks about Jesus, though he still believed they were true. Afterwards he broke down in tears. (Of course, John's suggestion that the group would overtake Christianity in popularity was never meant literally – though today, interestingly enough, a Google internet search yields slightly more hits for 'Beatles' than for 'Jesus'.) After the group finally got home, Brian Epstein conceded that their touring days were over, though he secretly went on making lists of venues for possible future concerts.

Reality leaves a lot to the imagination[221]

Head in the Clouds

'**A**fter we stopped touring, it always seemed embarrassing,' John remembered. 'Should we have dinner together? It always got so formal that none of us wanted to go through with it any more. When you don't see someone for a few months, you feel stilted and you have to start again.'[222] John's next project was to give him a dramatic way of starting again. After flying to Germany in September to start filming *How I Won the War*, he had his hair cut short for the part. (The clippings were burnt to thwart souvenir hunters, but the ashes were sold anyway.) It was more than just a cosmetic transformation. This was really the moment when Beatle John, the leader of the 'Fab Four', finally disappeared from view. After the film he would carry on wearing his round Private Gripweed 'granny' glasses too. In 'before and after' photographs it is difficult to see the old John Lennon behind the new one. From now on radical changes in his appearance would be a feature of his life: with each change he would seem to put the old persona behind him and begin anew.

Filming continued in Spain, where John shared a little house in Almeria with Michael Crawford. There he wrote something that would have been inconceivable even a year before: 'Strawberry Fields Forever'. For this song, which now seems one of his greatest, he used the name of the Woolton orphanage where he had trespassed as a boy to convey a trippy image of an elysian state of mind. The final version would begin with the words 'Let me take you down, 'cos I'm going to Strawberry Fields',[223] but John's original impulse was the more evocative 'Let me take you back . . .'.[224] '"Strawberry Fields" was psychoanalysis set to music, really,' he would later comment. 'I haven't met anybody that isn't a complete blockage of pain, from childhood, from birth on. Why shouldn't we cry? They tell us to stop crying about twelve: "Be a man." What the hell's that? Men hurt.'[225]

Then on 24 November 1966 it was into the EMI studio in Abbey Road for the first day of one of the most celebrated recording projects in the history of music, the 700-hour sessions for 'Sgt Pepper's Lonely Hearts Club Band'. George Martin would recall that though the Beatles' aim had once been to capture on record the sound of a live performance, they were now 'putting something down on tape that could only be done on tape.'[226] For example, 'Being For The Benefit Of Mr Kite!' (whose lyrics John had taken almost word for word from an 1843 circus poster) would have been difficult and unconvincing on stage, since much of the steam-organ backing track was generated from pieces of tape randomly spliced together.

Though they still liked having number one singles, the important musical medium for the Beatles was now the album. It was Paul who wanted to make this one more than just another collection of new tracks. Impressed by 'Pet Sounds', Brian Wilson's recent masterpiece with the Beach Boys, he envisaged a suite of songs linked in some way to the group's shared Liverpool roots. To start the ball rolling he composed one inspired by some discarded verses from John's first draft of 'In My Life'. These began: 'Penny Lane is one I'm missing', and went on to mention 'the 5 bus into town', 'Church Road', 'the tramsheds with no trams', and other places John remembered.[227] Paul, who called his Liverpool song simply 'Penny Lane', intended it to complement John's 'Strawberry Fields Forever' as the twin starting points for the new album. Unfortunately, when Brian Epstein heard them, he demanded that both tracks should be issued on a double A side single, which came out in February 1967.

As the Beatles disliked duplication, the album project had to start again, and everyone contributed an unlinked mix of songs as usual. Paul still wanted to impose some sort of shape, however. '"Sgt Pepper" is Paul, after a trip to America,' John recalled. 'The whole West Coast long-named group thing was coming in, when people were no longer The Beatles or The Crickets – they were suddenly Fred and His Incredible Shrinking Grateful Airplanes. I think he got influenced by that.'[228] It was Neil Aspinall, the Beatles' first roadie and now an indispensable companion, who revived the concept album idea by suggesting that the introductory 'Sgt Pepper' song should be reprised near the end, making the whole thing appear to be a concert staged by a fictional band. John approved of the idea, paying Neil a typically wry compliment: 'Nobody likes a smart-arse.'[229] Later, though, he would be more sceptical about the album's overall structure: '"Sgt Pepper" is called the first concept album, but it doesn't go anywhere. All my contributions to the album have absolutely nothing to do with the idea of Sgt Pepper and his band.'[230]

Though he enjoyed the 'Sgt Pepper' recording sessions, John was aware that he was not pulling his weight as a composer. He contributed only three full songs of his own, 'Mr Kite', 'Lucy In The Sky With Diamonds' and 'Good Morning, Good Morning', an underrated song which observed the quotidian horrors of family life in suburban Britain: though nothing ever seems to be happening, the hidden reality is that one must kill or be killed. However, despite a marked ceding of responsibility to Paul, John's gritty input was crucial throughout 'Sgt Pepper', both verbally and musically, and helped to bring a sense of unity to the whole album. He made telling additions to several of Paul's lyrics, among them 'What do you see when you turn out the light? I can't tell you but I know it's mine', in 'With A Little Help From My Friends', as well as suggesting the grim trio of grandchildren, 'Vera, Chuck and Dave', in 'When I'm Sixty-Four'. He also supplied the lines about cruelty to women for 'It's Getting Better' (and the inspired aside, 'It can't get no worse!')[231]

Many people regard the album's great climax, 'A Day In The Life', as the masterpiece of Lennon-McCartney collaboration. It opens with two episodes of dream, or nightmare, from John: one crowd of people passively observes a routine death in a car accident – 'Well I just had to laugh'; another crowd is too squeamish to watch a war film – 'But I just had to look.' This then gives way to Paul's jaunty description of humdrum, unthinking daily life – alarm clock, get up, cup of tea for breakfast, to work on the bus, with no suspicion of the terrifying complexity of life just below the surface. Then the song returns to John, who has spotted a strange news item about '4,000 holes in Blackburn, Lancashire'. Is this fact perhaps linked to the search for the murdered children buried on the moors, we wonder? No, it seems not, but it's the same number of holes as there are seats in the Albert Hall. The connections, John implies, are everywhere. They are complex, but they can be understood if only we open our minds. While the song's 'message', 'I'd love to turn you on',[232] is of course a reference to cannabis and/or LSD, it is also more than that, something like a plea for us all to see through the illusions we are forced to accept, to recognize the daily compromises we make, and to face the reality that everything, in the end, is linked to everything else.

For all the apocalyptic weight of the famous final crescendo, recording it in front of guests such as Mick Jagger, Marianne Faithfull and Britain's version of Bob Dylan, Donovan, was one of the happiest Beatles occasions of all. Everyone, even the 40-piece orchestra, wore fancy dress. As Paul remembered afterwards, 'We wanted to make a happening happen, and it happened.'[233] John was in philosophical mood when the album was released on 1 June 1967: 'I've had a lot of time to think and only now am I beginning to realise many of the things I should have known years ago. I'm getting to understand my feelings. Don't forget that under this frilly shirt is a hundred-year-old man who's seen and done so much, but, at the same

'A hundred-year-old man who's seen and done so much,' at the party for the release of Sgt Pepper's...

time, knowing so little.'[234] The record, whose innovations included the lack of silent 'rills' between tracks, the gatefold sleeve and the inclusion of the lyrics on the back, became the icon of the age. Everyone pored over Peter Blake's cover, looking for their heroes clustered around what is presumably the grave of the old moptop Beatles – where were Elvis and Buddy Holly? (Not there for copyright reasons: apart from the Beatles themselves and Stuart Sutcliffe, the only pop

135

musicians were Bob Dylan and the vintage rock 'n' roller Dion.) Were those cannabis plants? (No, the house plant *Pilea cadierei*, or 'aluminium' plant – though Paul thought they were the more suitable *Peperomia*.) Was it true that Jesus and Hitler were both there, but hidden behind the Beatles themselves? (According to Peter Blake they were, because John had insisted; others said not.)

Over 1967's so-called 'Summer of Love', London's streets and squares would made strange by the sound of George's sitar or the carnival swirl of Mr Kite. Smoky air rich with joss or other oriental scents drifted from basement and attic windows in Chiswick and Clapham and Camberwell. At the Roundhouse, and in clubs like UFO, there were light shows and freaky music. Be-ins, smoke-ins and happenings were being held in Hyde Park or Alexandra Palace. The 'underground press' was beginning to bloom, notably *International Times* and its friendly rival, Richard Neville's *Oz*, while in the USA, Jann Wenner would start *Rolling Stone* in October. (John read all these 'alternative' publications, and would later help *IT* financially.) Allen Ginsberg was in town, reading his poetry in the Indica bookshop (where John Lennon bought his books), and chanting mantras at Speaker's Corner. Along the Kings Road, Carnaby Street and Portobello Road, Nigel Waymouth and dozens of other laid-back capitalists opened and closed poster shops, boutiques, and loud pavement cafés with curious names. Procul Harum's 'A Whiter Shade Of Pale', a favourite 'tripping song' of John's, was number one in the charts in June; it gave way in July to his own 'All You Need Is Love', which was in turn ousted by 'San Francisco (Be Sure To Wear Flowers In Your Hair)' by Scott McKenzie in August. Ten years later Kenneth Tynan would be widely quoted as believing that 'Sgt Pepper' had been a decisive moment in the history of Western civilisation.

One afternoon in Hyde Park a Rolls Royce, decorated like a carnival ride and eccentrically fitted with external loudspeakers, silently drew up behind the Austin Princess belonging to Brian Jones of the Rolling Stones. The words

136

'Pull over now! Brian Jones! You are under arrest!'[235] rang out. It was just John and Paul's little joke, as Brian discovered when he saw them making v-signs out the windows at him, but it almost did for him. All over London the police were cracking down on rock stars with drugs. The BBC had banned 'A Day In The Life' for using the phrase 'I'd love to turn you on'. However, they were happy to broadcast the Beatles at the end of June as Britain's entry in an international TV programme, *Our World*. Resplendent in their multicoloured hippie gear, beads and moustaches, the band (they were no longer, it seems, a 'group') played 'All You Need Is Love', which John had written for the occasion. George Harrison would call the song 'a subtle bit of PR for God.'[236] In a silk coat painted with large eyes, Mick Jagger (who John once called 'the Charlie Chaplin of rock 'n' roll'),[237] was seen by 350 million people smoking a joint as he joined in the choruses. He was due in court the next day on drugs charges. Strange days indeed.

In late summer, after a lecture in the London Hilton, John and Cynthia met one of George Harrison's growing army of gurus, the Maharishi Mahesh Yogi, purveyor of Spiritual Regeneration, a bespoke brand of Transcendental Meditation. He gave them each 'a personal mantra in exchange for a clean white handkerchief, three pieces of fruit, and – last but not least – a full week's wages.'[238] Afterwards, Cynthia was puzzled by a funny little Japanese woman, apparently an avant-garde artist called Yoko Ono, who cadged a lift with them back to her flat, but remained silent all the way. On 25 August, John and the other Beatles set off by rail to Bangor, North Wales, to spend the weekend meditating at the Maharishi's feet. Mick Jagger, who had been sentenced to three months but released on appeal after a nationwide debate on cannabis, was with them, but not Cynthia Lennon. Mistaken for a fan at Euston Station, she had failed to get through the crowds in time, vainly cantering along the platform to John's encouraging shouts of 'Run, Cynthia! Run!' from the window of his departing train.[239] She had to follow by car. In Bangor, the press was

John and Cynthia photographed leaving Brian Epstein's funeral

informed that all the Beatles had now given up drugs. John told a reporter 'We don't regret taking drugs but we realise that if we'd met Maharishi before we had taken LSD, we would not have needed to take it.'[240] His large stock of liquid lysergic acid at home had not been thrown away, however, but lay buried in the garden at Kenwood.

Now that his four boys had stopped touring, Brian Epstein's role as their surrogate father had changed. He no longer really knew what he was meant to be doing. Though in public he still seemed calm and efficient, in reality his life had been in mounting disarray. Earlier in the year a psychiatrist had named his main problems as 'insomnia, agitation, anxiety and depression'.[241] To the list might be added sexual desperation. Earlier in August, when an interviewer asked his greatest fear, he replied, 'Loneliness. I hope I'll never be lonely, although, actually, one inflicts loneliness on oneself to a certain extent.'[242]

When the news came to Bangor it was a bad shock: Brian had been found dead on his bed, surrounded by bottles of pills. 'I introduced Brian to pills – which gives me a guilt association with his death – to make him talk, to find out what he was like,'[243] John would say much later. The coroner blamed alcohol and a build-up of barbiturates. Despite predictable rumours of suicide or murder, his death had probably been an accident waiting to happen. He had been taking all the drugs the Beatles had been taking, and more. John remembered the Maharishi's reaction: 'We went to him and he was, sort of, saying, '"Oh, forget it, be happy, like an idiot, like parents, smile." That's what Maharishi said, and we did!'[244] In 1970 John revealed how much the loss had really worried him: it had felt almost like the death of a parent. 'I knew we were in trouble then. I didn't really have any misconceptions about our ability to do anything other than play music and I was scared. I thought, "We've fuckin' had it."'[245]

A few days after Brian's death, perhaps at the prompting of Hunter Davies (then researching his authorized Beatle biography), a letter of sympathy came from John's real father, who was currently washing dishes in a hotel not far from Weybridge. It may have been the benign influence of the Maharishi, or the sense of oneness with the universe that LSD had brought to John's expanded mind, or simply

139

because a summer cloud of love and peace seemed to have descended on everyone, but John replied at once in the friendliest terms (to 'Dear Alf, Fred, Dad, Pater whatever'). After their last encounter, when John had slammed the door on him, Freddie's brother Charlie had explained by letter that it was actually John's mother who had broken up the marriage, first by getting pregnant and then by going off with Dykins. Hunter Davies too was now relaying Freddie's side of the story to John, the trip to Blackpool and all. 'I know it will be a bit awkward when we first meet and maybe for a few meetings,' wrote John in his letter to his father, 'but there's hope for us yet.' He asked Freddie not to tell the press that they would be getting together: 'I don't want Mimi cracking up!'[246]

Events since Brian's death would vindicate John's fears about the future of the Beatles. Though Paul kept them all working, nothing was now quite the same. They recorded songs for his latest brainchild, a musical film for television called *Magical Mystery Tour*. The whole venture was planned on the hop. 'We haven't got a script yet,' said John, 'but we've got a bloke going round the lavatories of Britain, cribbing all the notes off the walls.'[247] John wrote a single scene for the movie, involving himself, a fat lady, spaghetti and a shovel. He also contributed one song, 'I Am The Walrus'. It was one of his masterpieces.

Like many Lennon creations, the song's origins went back to his early reading – the Walrus and the Eggman (Humpty Dumpty) both come from Lewis Carroll. But there was another link with John's childhood too. In the summer of 1967, a pupil at Quarry Bank, Stephen Bayley, had written to him, mentioning that the songs of the Beatles were being analysed in his English class. Pete Shotton was there when John opened the letter, and the two old Quarry Men were much amused. John decided on the spot to compose a song that would defy any teacher's powers of analysis. For the first verse of this very atmospheric English fantasy, he adapted a playground song they both remembered – 'Yellow matter custard dripping from a dead dog's eye.' Elsewhere he threw in portmanteau words, Buddhist sayings, references to other Beatles songs and the most ludicrous images his imagination could conjure: 'Let the fuckers work that one out, Pete.'[248] As for a tune, when a police car drove past, its 'nee-naw' siren blaring, the song was off: 'I am he as you are he as you are me as we are all together . . .'[249] On 1 September, young Stephen Bayley was rewarded with a chatty reply from John, who signed off 'Love, (No, Aim not queer!) John Lennon.'[250] Less than a week later John brought the finished song to the studio for the new film.

During the ad hoc editing process of *Magical Mystery Tour*, John said 'Film making isn't as difficult as many people imagine. It's a matter of common sense more than anything . . . *Magical Mystery Tour* was an experiment and, so far, it's been successful.'[251] Not for much longer. On 26 December the film was broadcast on BBC1. Partly (but not entirely) because it was shown in black and white, it received almost universal ridicule from the critics, and even fans were disappointed. As a period piece, the virtues of the film are more apparent today, not least its striking visual effects and the Beatles' delightfully innocent approach to cinematic technique. At the time, however, it looked as if the desire for excellence that had driven the group from triumph to successive triumph was draining away.

Draining away even more rapidly was the Beatles' money. Though they were generating more income than ever, most of their earnings were crippled by a 96 per cent tax burden under Wilson's Labour government. Something had to be done, but with no manager, there was nobody to make a decision except the Beatles themselves, and they, to put it mildly, were inclined at times to be irrational. In Neil Aspinall's words, 'Suddenly the lunatics had got hold of the asylum.'[252] Various schemes, each more utopian than the last, were being considered. The Beatles very nearly bought an island in Greece, and thought of living there permanently, repelling all uninvited guests as they dreamed their grassy dreams. (John had already bought himself two off the west coast of Ireland, but he hadn't even visited them yet.) They

141

discussed building a stately pleasure dome, perhaps in Norfolk, with mansions around it for each Beatle and comfortable family dwellings nearby for their favoured inner circle. 'Wars, nationalism, fascism, communism, capitalism, nastiness, religion – none of it works,' said John. 'So why not this?'[253] Finally they revived an idea that had been floated before Brian's death, and agreed to sink cash into a new umbrella organization, called Apple Corps, which would spend the Beatles' money in ways they approved of, before it reached the taxman. John succinctly summed up the scheme: 'It's a business concerning records, films, and electronics and, as a sideline, manufacturing, or whatever.'[254] Apple's first venture was a boutique in Baker Street, selling clothes and anything else that caught their fancy. Pete Shotton, who since 1965 had been successfully running a supermarket that John had bought for him, was put in charge, and the shop opened on 5 December with a great party, at which apple juice was served. It was to close only eight months later.

Freddie Lennon had by now met John and had stayed, rather awkwardly, for some weeks at Kenwood, getting to know his son properly again. He was currently living near Kew in a house bought for him by John, who paid him a modest weekly allowance. Now 54, he had acquired a girlfriend of 19, Pauline Jones, calling her 'Polly' after his mother, though he told John that she looked more like Julia. Soon she was working in Kenwood, babysitting Julian and doing secretarial work for John. Freddie and John got drunk together one night, at a fancy dress ball to celebrate *Magical Mystery Tour*. John was in Teddy boy gear and his old man wore the unwashed clothes of a friendly, if aromatic, dustman he had met. On the drive home, John laid his head in Freddie's lap and allowed him to stroke the back of his neck. It was as close as the two would ever get.

After Pauline became pregnant in the spring, the couple moved to Brighton to get away from journalists

Left to right: Cynthia Lennon, Jane Asher, Paul McCartney, Donovan, Mia Farrow, George Harrison, the Maharishi, Mike Love, John Lennon, and Patti Boyd in Rishikesh

scenting scandal. There John would buy them a house for £6,500. In due course they married, and Freddie became a proper father at last, pushing the prams of his two little sons and changing their nappies. But despite pious promises, there were no visits from his eldest. When Hunter Davies's biography of the Beatles came out in September 1968, Freddie was horrified find that Mimi's version of events had been favoured over his. In 1970, John would say about the book: 'no home truths were written, my auntie knocked all the truth bits from my childhood and my mother out and I allowed it . . .'[255]

On 15 February 1968, John and Cynthia flew out

to India. With the other Beatles they planned to stay for three months in Rishikesh under the guidance of the Maharishi, with no drink, no drugs, and since they were no longer sleeping together, no sex. 'He made us live in separate huts from our wives . . . Can't say it was too much of a strain,' John laconically commented later.[256] At the first lesson, as Donovan would recall, 'there was an embarrassing silence. It was just the four Beatles, Mia Farrow, Mike Love and myself . . . John was so funny and so direct that, to break the silence, he went up to Maharishi, who was sitting cross-legged on the floor, patted him on the head, and said, "'There's a good little Guru!"'[257] In Rishikesh, John worked his way up to eight hours' meditation a day. 'That was the competition in Maharishi's camp,' he would recall in 1980, 'who was going to get cosmic first. (What I didn't know was I was already cosmic.)'[258] He found it difficult to sleep, and spent much of his time writing 'I'm So Tired' and about a dozen other songs, most destined for the double album the Beatles would begin when they got home. He was waiting for the Maharishi to give him 'the secret', a formula that he was convinced would be imparted to him when the time was right. But John already had a secret of his own, carefully kept from Cynthia: whenever he had not emptied his mind for meditation purposes, it was occupied by Yoko Ono. Four days before they had gone to Rishikesh, he had invited her to witness the recording of a new song of his in the studio, 'Hey Bulldog'. She had failed to endear herself to the band by wondering why the Beatles always used such simple rhythms. Now, unknown to Cynthia, the morning post was bringing John a shoal of letters and notes from her, with further useful advice: 'Keep Laughing For A Week', 'Hit A Wall With Your Head',[259] or more intimately, 'I'm a cloud. Watch for me in the sky.'[260]

The previous October John had put up money for her 'Half-Wind Show: Yoko Plus Me' at the Lisson Gallery, though he hadn't gone to see the display of washbasins, toothbrushes, pillows etc, all neatly cut in half and painted white. While intimates knew that 'Me' was John Lennon, his involvement was officially anonymous. The pair had first met at another show in November 1966, when John had offered the artist an imaginary five shillings to hammer an imaginary nail into one of her exhibits, and their eyes had met. (The story of this first encounter would become part of their shared mythology, honed by both of them in innumerable interviews.) John had been both intrigued and irritated by her book, *Grapefruit*, with its advice to 'Bleed', or to 'Hide until everybody goes home. Hide until everybody forgets about you. Hide until everybody dies.'[261] But he kept it by his bed.

When John heard rumours (apparently unfounded) that the Maharishi had designs not only on the souls of some of the female pilgrims, but on their bodies as well, he told him he was leaving. '"Why?" he asked, and I said, "If you're so cosmic, you'll know why!"'[262] On the way to the airport John began a new song, singing 'Maharishi, what have you done? You made a fool of everyone.'[263] It would appear on their forthcoming double album, with the name prudently changed to 'Sexy Sadie'. On the plane back from India on 12 April he shocked Cynthia by telling her for the first time that he had not been entirely faithful during their marriage, though there was no mention of Yoko. Back home, he dug up his stash and went back to LSD, tripping and smoking dope as much as ever. He encouraged Cynthia to go off to Greece for a holiday, and seemed too preoccupied when she left even to say goodbye. The day before her return, after an evening on acid with Pete Shotton, John called a board meeting at the Apple HQ. 'I've something very important to tell you all,' he announced to the other Beatles and their senior staff, 'I am . . . Jesus Christ come back again.'[264] It was tactfully decided that perhaps it might be best to take no immediate action on the matter. Later the same day, John phoned Yoko from Kenwood and invited her round. They made beautiful electronic music together all night.

Half of what I say

is meaningless . . .

265

Little Acorns

Yoko Ono was seven years older than John Lennon. She had been born in Japan in 1933, daughter of a concert pianist turned banker. During her childhood the family was often in the USA. She studied philosophy in a Japanese university before going to college in New York, where she married a young Japanese composer. They returned to Japan in the early 1960s. While in the throes of a mental breakdown, she met Tony Cox, a musician and film-maker, who became her second husband. Their daughter, Kyoko, was born in 1963. Back in New York, Yoko became a conceptual artist with the Fluxus collective, largely dependent on rich sponsors to fund her 'happenings'. Then in 1966 Tony Cox was offered free use of a flat in London, and they arrived in England. Since then, Yoko had been tirelessly working to make a name on the British modern art scene, though with little success.

When Cynthia got back from her holiday in Greece, she found John and Yoko still together in the house. Rattled, she invited them both to come out to dinner with friends, and when they politely declined, she picked up her bags, turned on her heel and left. John and Cynthia would be divorced in November.

In 1968, politics were everywhere. Even the Beatles' cartoon film, *Yellow Submarine*, premiered in July, was seen as carrying a subliminal political message, pitting the capitalist 'Blue Meanies' against the four devil-may-care individualist Beatles – though as Paul would say, in fact the Beatles deserved as little credit for it as the seven dwarfs did for *Snow White*. John's political sympathies had for some time been drifting to the left. In 1967, during the week that 'Sgt Pepper' was released, a television adaptation was shown on BBC2 of *The Ragged Trousered Philanthropists*, by Robert Tressell, an angry fictional exploration of the war between the classes in Britain. John, whose house was stuffed with electronic gadgets, must have had some sort of early home video equipment for, according to Derek Taylor, then the Apple press agent, John was so impressed by the programme 'that he watched a recording of it over and over again on his new fangled machine'.[266]

Robert Tressell was a pseudonym. His ancestry, like John Lennon's, is lost in the mists of Irish history. His family seem to have been middle-class Dubliners, but he died in Liverpool of tuberculosis in 1911, and was buried there in a pauper's grave. Tressell adopted the cause of the working man, earning a living as a jobbing housepainter and signwriter, and working on his novel in his spare time. The title of his book summed up his position: the working classes were his 'ragged trousered philanthropists'. Like impoverished and perverse charitable benefactors they donated the fruits of their labour to their rich bosses, getting only meagre wages and no thanks in return. When it was published posthumously in 1914, Tressell became the original 'working class hero'; his book went through many editions and became a standard text in the strengthening Labour Party – for which it was popularly said to have won the 1945 General Election. Alan Sillitoe, in his introduction to the book's 1965 edition, remarks 'Those whose life has touched the misery recounted by Robert Tressell can get out of it many things: a bolstering of class feeling; pure rage; reinforcement for their own self-pity; a call to action; maybe a good and beneficial dose of all these things.'[267] Though John's encounter with *The Ragged Trousered Philanthropists* (initially at least) was through television, Tressell's uncompromising message would leave an indelible mark on him.

From now on, John and Yoko were almost never seen apart, a unit both in public and in private. They became 'johnandyoko'.[268] While he was with Cynthia, as he later recalled, 'I'd get fed up every now and then, and I'd start this "where is she?" bit. I'd hope that the "one" would come . . . I suppose I was hoping for a woman who could give me what I got from a man, intellectually. I wanted someone I could be myself with.'[269] Yoko was the dream woman that John had always been waiting for, the one he had sung about in songs like 'Yes It Is', 'Girl' and 'Lucy In The Sky With Diamonds'. For the first time he had someone close to him who would listen with loving enthusiasm to his thoughts, his obsessions, even his politics. Yoko may not have altered John's political opinions very much, but she helped him to act upon them in public. Through the example of her confrontational art, he would find ways not only to express his beliefs as they evolved, but to get them widely publicized as well. Their first, and most famous, project together was ambitious: to bring about world peace.

A shockingly realistic film by Peter Watkins, *The War Game*, was currently making pacifists of much of the left in Britain. In a letter, Watkins persuaded John that his fame and influence could and should be exploited for this most important of political ends. John was aware that peace was a cause that chimed oddly with his natural inclinations: 'I know how I felt when I was at college at 19 or 20 – I would have been for complete destruction.'[270] In his private life too he had often been more aggressive than eirenic. But since John was viscerally opposed to what he saw as the hypocrisy and elitism of western capitalist governments, which were all currently implicated, actively or passively, in war and injustice of every sort, his stance on peace was in fact also a position of combative opposition: 'I think

George, Ringo, Yoko, John and Paul, displaying the high spirits that prevailed during the making of 'Let It Be'

our society is run by insane people for insane objectives and I sussed that when I was 16 . . .'[271] He had long been consistent in his hostility to military conflict. On their 1966 tour of the USA, the Beatles had answered questions about Vietnam in unison: 'We don't like war, war is wrong.'[272] John had made his most powerful early pacifist statement at the premiere of *How I Won the War* in 1967, during a week when 100,000 people had marched on the Pentagon in protest against US involvement in Vietnam: 'I hate war. If there is another war I won't fight and I'll try to tell all the youngsters not to fight either. I hate all the sham.'[273]

John knew that he was not alone: all the 'tuned in, turned on' generation agreed with him already, all the hippies, the flower power heads, the dope smokers, the artists, the poets, the musicians, most of the students. He just had to convert the rest of the young to peace, and time would do the rest. Yoko had already made a film for peace called *Bottoms*, in which 365 people had 'signed' a peace petition by baring their buttocks to camera, and she was happy to go all the way with John on this. Her input helped to crystallise his thoughts: they could combine his Beatle celebrity with her conceptual art skills to launch an enormous advertising drive for peace. His experience on the wrong side of the 'bigger than Jesus' debate had demonstrated how quickly public opinion could be manipulated: his opinions, if they were striking enough, would be heard around the world. 'The only way to ensure a lasting peace of any kind is to change people's minds. The Government can do it with propaganda, Coca-Cola can do it with propaganda – why can't we?'[274]

First, however, there was business to attend to, a Beatles album to be made, and at the end of May 1968, the group was back at work, recording the songs that they had written in Rishikesh. The process would take five months, and John kept Yoko with him in the studio throughout, though she was there distinctly on sufferance. The first song they tackled was 'Revolution'. John wrote it while students on the streets of Paris were igniting a general workers' strike that for a while seemed likely to reshape French democracy. 'Revolution' had two versions. On the single, as B side to Paul's anthem, 'Hey Jude', it was sung fast, to fiercely distorted guitars. This dirty, uncompromising music sounded like a call for violent revolution; but the words said quite the opposite:

'Well, you know, we all want to change the world, But when you talk about destruction, Don't you know that you can count me out?'[275] The revolutionary left, both in England and the USA, was scathing about the perceived weakness of John's position. To an attack in the radical magazine, *Black Dwarf*, he responded: 'I don't worry about what you, the left, the middle, the right or any fucking boys club think. I'm not that bourgeois. . . . I'm not only up against the establishment but you too. . . . I'll tell you what's wrong with the world: people – so do you want to destroy them? Unless you / we change our heads – there's no chance.'[276] On the album, when it appeared in November, the song (retitled 'Revolution 1') was played slower, allowing its message to be heard more clearly, but it was even more ambiguous: the left noticed that John's opinion of destruction seemed to have changed: now after 'count me out' he could also be heard singing the word 'in'.[277] When Tariq Ali asked him about this in 1971, he replied, disarmingly, 'I put both in as I wasn't sure.'[278]

In June, the 1968 National Sculpture Exhibition was held in the shell of old Coventry Cathedral, which had been left ruined as a memorial to German bomb casualties. Grudgingly allowed to take part, John and Yoko planted two 'peace acorns' to symbolize 'the East and West coming together.'[279] They issued an explanatory leaflet stating 'This is what happens when two clouds meet,'[280] but the cathedral's Canon Verney refused to distribute it as the clouds in question were not married; John told him witheringly that 'Jesus would have loved our piece for what it IS.'[281] The acorns were dug up by fans within a week, and had to be replaced and guarded. This opening event in their long drive for peace would be a model for many future joint ventures.

The previous year, John had eventually visited Dorinish, the linked pair of small uninhabited islands that he had bought off the west coast of County Mayo. Surrounded by the breathtaking scenery of Clew Bay, Dorinish had a natural harbour, a 98-foot cliff populated by seabirds, a

154

maze of paths made by the sheep that were grazed there, and very little else. A local boatbuilder, Paddy Quinn, sailed him out to look at it one afternoon. Afterwards he took John for a cup of tea on his own island, Ballycuttle, where Quinn's dog, Sandy, attacked his 'hairy' coat. 'It was only afterwards that I discovered it was John Lennon,' Quinn would recall. 'Beatlemania and the Swinging Sixties had not quite reached the west of Ireland.'[282] Planning permission for a house was quickly granted, but for the meantime, Julian's celebrated psychedelic gypsy caravan was brought to Ireland, and one calm summer's evening it was floated out to the island on a specially-built raft, a sight that is still remembered locally.

Now, a year later, on 22 June, John whisked Yoko, Pete Shotton and three or four others off to Dorinish. They landed by helicopter and ate a meal in the now rather damp caravan, before venturing out to explore the first Lennon property in Ireland for at least a century. After a night in the relative comfort of the hotel in nearby Mulranny, they spent a day sightseeing by car. A reporter for the *Mayo News*, amazed to find himself interviewing John Lennon and 'his Japanese lady friend Joko Ono' (sic), wrote that the 'Beatle Millionaire' was 'enchanted' by the countryside: 'The fact that the area is in no way commercialised adds to its beauty,' John apparently told him.[283] But though that was to be John's last sight of Ireland, he was never to forget about this symbolic foothold in his ancestral land. In 1969 he would lend the island to Sid Rawle, 'King of the Hippies', who founded a commune of tent-dwellers there (optimistically called 'The Children of the Sun'). They stayed in dwindling numbers until 1973, when the last of their tents burned down during a storm.

Back in London, John's first art exhibition, entitled 'You Are Here', was about to open at the Robert Fraser Gallery in Duke Street. At the launch, as 365 white helium balloons were released to spread the word, John announced: 'I declare the balloons . . . high!'[284] Inside, spectators were greeted with a round white painting bearing the words *you*

155

are here, words that were 'aimed directly at the spectators, informing them that they were at Lennon's exhibition, in front of his round painting' (as a critic would helpfully explain in 1995).[285] Life-size models of crippled children dominated the exhibition's collection of collection boxes for various charities, which included the artist's own collection box, an inverted white hat, marked *For the Artist. Thank you*.[286] John was delighted when someone sarcastically donated a rusty bicycle for him to display as well, and he promptly did so. The exhibition was largely ignored by the modern art establishment, because it was by a Beatle, and by Beatle fans, because it was modern art.

John and Yoko also became experimental movie makers. One of their first was *Film No. 5 – Smile*, a three-minute portrayal of John breaking into a smile, filmed on a very high-speed camera. Projected over 50 minutes, it was intended, Yoko said, 'for people who'd like to have the film on their wall as a light portrait'. 'The idea of the film won't really be dug for another 50 or 100 years,' said John.[287] In August, *Private Eye* reported the words of 'Yoko Hana': 'We've started to make lots of films together. There's this one of him sitting in a chair picking his nose. Every so often he gives a little gurk'.[288] Personally, John was amused to be one of the magazine's targets, and over the next few years he would make many appearances in its pages as 'Comrade Spiggy Topes', the right-on pop singer and apologist for international socialism.

By the autumn of 1968 it was clear that the hippie dream was not going to take over the world. In June assassin's bullets had killed Bobby Kennedy, and had seriously wounded Andy Warhol; in August the USSR had invaded Czechoslovakia; in October Tommy Smith made his Black Power salute on the Olympic podium; Richard Nixon became US President in November.

For John and Yoko too, it was a horrible autumn. They were now living in squalor (though hardly poverty) in Ringo's old London flat. John was hurt and baffled by the racist and sexist abuse being poured over them at home

Busted! John and Yoko are hustled out of their court hearing

and internationally in the press. It was becoming open season on Yoko: soon, *Esquire*, for example, would headline an article about her 'John Rennon's Excrusive Gloupie'.[289] They were now snorting heroin together – Yoko had been already flirting with it for some months. On the 1968 Beatles' annual Christmas flexidisc for fan club members John would later blame the press for their drug use, though he expressed it so enigmatically that nobody noticed: 'Being in love they cloong even more together man – but some of the poisonessmonster of outrated buslodedshithrowers did stick slightly and they occasionally had to resort to the drycleaners. Luckily this did not kill them and they werent banned from the olympic games.'[290] In October, despite being warned that the police were on the way, they were busted, and charged with possession of a small lump of cannabis. Within a day, Yoko, who was due to give birth in February, was rushed to hospital with a threatened miscarriage: despite emergency blood transfusions she would lose the baby a month later. At the trial on 28 November, John pleaded guilty in exchange for immunity for Yoko, fearing she would be deported. He received a £150 fine and a criminal record. John believed that he had been targeted because he was a 'loudmouth'[291] and that the dope had been planted. 'The Beatles thing was over. No reason to protect us for being soft and cuddly any more – so bust us!'[292] He may have been right: Detective Sergeant Pilcher, the officer in charge of the operation, was already notorious, and would eventually be caught and imprisoned for planting evidence. John and Yoko would always blame the authorities for the loss of their first child.

On 29 November Apple released 'Unfinished Music No. 1 – Two Virgins', an extract from the freeform 'music' which the couple had recorded on that first night together in Kenwood. Amid the strange sounds and bodily noises were snatches of conversation – John: 'It's just me, Hilda, I'm home for tea.' Yoko: 'Tea's never ready.' Some words of Paul McCartney, possibly inspired by the meeting of clouds mentioned in the 'Acorn Peace' leaflet, appeared under one of the photographs, though quite what he meant remains in doubt: 'When two great Saints meet it is a humbling experience. The long battles to prove he was a Saint.' The album would probably have come and gone as quietly as the July art exhibition had it not been for its sleeve, which bore two grimy, full-length photographs of John and Yoko standing together in a messy bedroom, stark naked.

'I didn't think there'd be such a fuss,' John would

comment, 'I guess the world thinks we're an ugly couple.'[293] He explained the reasoning behind the photographs: 'If people can't face up to the fact of other people being naked or smoking pot, or whatever they want to do, then we're never going to get anywhere. Being ourselves is what's important.'[294] Elsewhere he expanded the point: 'If we can make society accept these kind of things without offence, without sniggering, then we shall be achieving our purpose. There has got to be law and order, but that doesn't mean we should suffer bad, out-of-date laws. If laws weren't changing they would still be jumping on queers and putting them away.[295]

The public was not convinced. No music papers would accept advertisements for the album, which eventually appeared in some record shops shrouded decently in brown paper bearing a Biblical quotation about the nakedness of Adam and Eve, though still many outlets refused to stock it. The one occasion that 'Two Virgins' would be heard on radio was after midnight on 12 December, a three-minute extract on John Peel's BBC programme *Night Ride*. The album sold only about 5,000 copies before being deleted. A year later John would ruefully reflect: 'She forced me to become avant-garde and take my clothes off, when all I wanted was to become Tom Jones.'[296]

At least the Beatles were still on track, more or less. On 22 November their double album, 'The Beatles' (which would universally come to be known as 'The White Album') was released, again containing nothing but original compositions. As well as 'Revolution 1' and 'Sexy Sadie', John had contributed eleven tracks, many of which sounded simpler and rawer than of late, a sign of his impatience with the nitpicking artifice that had produced 'Sgt Pepper'. Yoko's approach to her art had reminded him of the natural minimalism that had first attracted him to rock 'n' roll, of the value of inspiration rather than craft. Several of these songs, such as 'Yer Blues', 'I'm So Tired' and 'Glass Onion' (partly a caustic look at the Beatles themselves) were laced with ennui or cynical wit, but there

159

also were gentler guitar-based ballads like 'Dear Prudence' and 'Cry Baby Cry', and even a reasonably straight-faced schmaltzy lullaby sung by Ringo, 'Good Night', which John had written for Julian. 'Happiness Is A Warm Gun' was different, though: many hours of concentrated work from all four Beatles went into this rich, surreal composite of half-songs from Rishikesh, with lyrics so besmirched by sordid references to sexual symbols, heroin and Yoko Ono (as 'Mother Superior') that it would be banned by the BBC. And then there was 'Revolution 9', John's eight-minute 'abstract sound picture', or 'montage of feelings in sound'. It was based on a rejected early outro of 'Revolution', skilfully mixed with tape-loops and other piano and voice noodlings that he had done at various times with Pete Shotton, Yoko and George Harrison. He had to fight for space on the album for this chillingly successful portrait of a possible dystopian future: his success meant that the track, John Lennon's greatest experiment in 'cosmic meandering', as he called it,[297] could later be identified as 'the world's most widely distributed avant-garde artefact'.[298] But then, as John would quip, 'Avant-garde is French for bullshit.'[299]

John later called 'The White Album' his favourite Beatles LP. It was the first one that allowed his work to be heard exactly as he wished, without any compromises. The five-month recording process had been beset by tensions in the group. Even Ringo had withdrawn for a few days, thinking he wasn't needed. Since Brian's death they had all been finding Paul's managing attitude difficult to take, and recently had even suggested that he should get it out of his system by making a solo album: 'It was going to be called,' John said, '"Paul McCartney Goes Too Far".'[300] There were no Lennon-McCartney collaborations in the old sense at all on the album, and it contained no duets. Now it was easier than ever before to identify which of the Beatles had written which songs: on only about half the tracks did all four of them actually perform. However, in the end the music seemed to have suffered very little, and the group magic was recaptured again and again, partly thanks to the refreshing hint of self-parody that ran through all four sides of the album.

John's first entirely solo excursion on a Beatles record concludes the second side. 'Julia' was wholly serious, and so personal that some have felt that he originally intended not to include it at all: it was the last song to be recorded for 'The White Album'. Accompanying himself on finger-picked acoustic guitar (a technique learned from Donovan in Rishikesh), John opens with a line adapted from Kalil Gibran: 'Half of what I say is meaningless, but I say it just to reach you.' The song seems to introduce Julia Lennon to Yoko (whose name in Japanese is the song's 'ocean child'), and soon it is clear that the two most important women in his life have somehow psychically united in his heart. While this song of love and devotion is gentle and understated, the naked emotion it reveals points the way forward to John's searing encounters with himself and his past that would inspire his first post-Beatles compositions.

December brought a flurry of Yuletide events. On the 18th, John Lennon performed at the Royal Albert Hall for the first time since 15 September 1963, when the Beatles had been screamed at on the same bill as the Rolling Stones. This time, however, he appeared (or perhaps, failed to appear) inside a white bag with Yoko as part of the 'Alchemical Wedding', a festive underground 'happening'. It was the first of their 'bag-ins'. They rolled around on stage for 25 minutes to the sound of a flute, while a protestor in the audience waved a Biafran flag and yelled repeatedly, 'John Lennon, do you care about that?'[301] Less publicly, five days later the couple presided over the Apple Christmas party, a shambolic affair which was blighted by the presence of a small chapter of American Hell's Angels that nobody dared to get rid of. Pouring with sweat in Father and Mother Christmas costumes, the couple, strung out on heroin, distributed presents to any children they could find among the chaos. The occasion was an omen: the whole business side of the Beatles was in terminal disarray. Nothing that anyone could suggest would ever be able to clear it up again.

Give Peace a chance . . .
Kiss A Cop For Peace
Week! 302

He Bag Production[303]

John would spend 1969 further enmeshing his life with Yoko's and at the same time emotionally disengaging from the Beatles. His involvement in group projects was now decidedly half-hearted. The first six weeks of the year were spent back in the studio again, preparing an album of new material which they could then record live at a concert, perhaps on an ocean liner. Though this was an interesting idea, these long, unfocused rehearsals were, said John, 'the most miserable sessions on earth.'[304] Over 200 different songs, many of them half-remembered tunes from years before, were started, or partly played, but very few were finished. John thought the concert should be held in a lunatic asylum: 'I was stoned all the time, too, on H, etc,' he said later, 'I just didn't give a shit – nobody did.'[305] Lack of enthusiasm was the crucial factor in the debacle, but it was seriously compounded by the presence of Yoko, whose interventions in every aspect of their business, including the music, were driving the other Beatles mad.

Largely to fulfil a contractual obligation for a third Beatles feature film, the whole grisly process was captured on film and audio tape, thus preserving for posterity several acrimonious studio conversations. However, the worst conflict of all, on 10 January, was not caught on camera or microphone. Whatever it was that John said to George that day was never afterwards explained, but George quit the band at once. While he was gone, Yoko pointedly occupied his blue cushion, and John led the remaining Beatles into a spontaneous performance of the Who's 'A Quick One While He's Away'. A 'weird, angry'[306] jam session followed, to which Yoko contributed earsplittingly dissonant screechings of John's name. After this impromptu audition, John suggested that the new vacancy should be offered to Eric Clapton. In the end, however, George was coaxed back. An attenuated version of the planned concert was played one lunchtime at the end of the month on the freezing roof of the Apple building, overheard only by a puzzled crowd of office workers and passers-by in the street below. After extensive post-production tweaking by Phil Spector and others, songs from the performance, coupled with the best of what are really still rehearsal tapes, would eventually be released as the final Beatles album before the break-up, 'Let It Be'.

John's work was becoming ever more autobiographical. On 30 May 'The Ballad Of John And Yoko' was issued as the new Beatles single (though only John and Paul played on it). It chronicled the activities of John and Yoko over ten days in March: with both of their divorces now through, they had been 'married in Gibraltar (near Spain)', and then had revealed a new weapon in their 'peace offensive', which they called 'Bed Peace'. Though the media hoped that the newlyweds were going to put on an exhibition of lovemaking for everyone to tut at, in fact they merely invited the world's press to their honeymoon bedroom in an Amsterdam hotel to discuss why they were in bed. ('The newspapers said, "She's gone to his head – They look like two Gurus in drag".') Then they were off to Vienna for the TV premiere of their film, *Rape*, in which for a whole day a girl is followed around by a camera against her will. John and Yoko themselves avoided cameras by staying in a bag throughout the launch. (The bag was becoming their trademark: in April they set up a company, 'Bag

Productions', to organize their PR and financing.) Back home, during a ceremony held on the all-purpose roof of the Apple building, John completed the wedding by having his middle name officially changed from 'Winston' to 'Ono', reflecting his new feminist awareness.

As it gathered momentum, the peace campaign generated an enormous amount of publicity, much of it revealing a hostility that he was unused to. However, John considered ridicule in the press a price worth paying: 'Yoko and I are quite willing to be the world's clowns if by doing so it will do some good. I know I'm one of these "famous personalities". For reasons only known to themselves, people do print what I say. And I'm saying peace. We're not pointing a finger at anybody. There are no good guys and bad guys. The struggle is in the mind. We must bury our monsters and stop condemning people. We are all Christ and we are all Hitler. We want Christ to win. We're trying to make Christ's message contemporary. What would he have done if he had advertisements, records, films, TV and newspapers? Christ made miracles to tell his message. Well, the miracle today is communications, so let's use it.[307]

All that spring and summer John and Yoko refused to let the public off the hook. Soon after arriving back in England (where, somewhat unexpectedly, 'The men from the press said, "we wish you success, It's good to have the both of you back"'), they tried to send acorns to every world leader, suggesting that they all got together in a very large bag indeed and held a peace conference. Unfortunately, being springtime, acorns proved elusive, so Apple employees were instructed to place squirrels under surveillance in various London parks to find out where they had buried them. John was given a rough time on Eamonn Andrews' TV chat show, trying to explain 'bagism' to an unreceptive Jack Benny and fighting about pacifism with Yehudi Menuhin. People were beginning to say he had gone completely mad. 'Christ! You know it ain't easy, You know how hard it can be. The way things

John and Yoko sharing a bed with Eamonn Andrews

are going, They're gonna crucify me.'[308] Mimi's view was that John was just being naughty as usual.

On 9 May the couple's second album was released: 'Unfinished Music No 2: Life With The Lions'. On one side was a live free-form jazz gig recorded at a March concert in Cambridge, featuring a selection of Yoko's best yells backed by feedback noises from John's guitar; the other included the only performance ever given by their unborn son, John Ono Lennon II, a five minute *in utero* recording of his heartbeats made in hospital by his father.

168

The record sleeve showed Yoko in her hospital bed, with John on a mattress on the floor beside her, and this time it was good old George Martin who supplied the sleeve endorsement: 'No comment'.[309] Later in the year there would be a third album in the series, called 'Wedding Album', with further aural curiosities including chat from the Amsterdam bed-in and even a few spontaneous songs, packaged in an elaborate box that contained a photograph of a slice of wedding cake (in a bag, naturally) and other unlikely goodies.

'We are both artists,' said John. 'Peace is our art.'[310] They were soon off again on a ten-day peace junket, to Canada via Bermuda – John was having difficulty getting a visa for the USA because of his drug conviction. In a Montreal hotel for their second bed-in, John gave over 60 press interviews, and spent much of the time on the telephone to radio stations, urging peace. On 1 June, in bed with his wife and his guitar, he recorded a new campaign song. His backing choir included Allen Ginsberg, Derek Taylor, an ecstatic Timothy Leary, Petula Clark, the American comedian Tommy Smothers, the Canadian Chapter of the Radha Krishna Temple and a couple of dozen other passing friends. Percussion was supplied by Yoko on wardrobe. 'Give Peace A Chance' would be out as a single within a month, credited to Lennon-McCartney as usual, but it was not released as a Beatles song. Instead, John and Yoko had come up with yet another new idea.

This was the 'Plastic Ono Band'. It was all explained at the record's launch in Chelsea Town Hall, where four perspex containers holding electronic equipment had been arranged centre stage. John was not present, though he later described the scene: 'All the press came to meet the band, and the band was on stage, which was just a machine with a camera pointing at them, showing them on stage themselves. So the Plastic Ono Band is a conceptual band that never was. There never had been any members in it, and the advert said, "You are the Plastic Ono

Band".'[311] In reality, of course, 'Give Peace A Chance' was John Lennon's first solo single. With a simple chorus written specifically for use as a peace anthem, it called on everyone to forget their differences ('Bagism, Shagism, Dragism, Madism, Ragism, Tagism, Thisism, Thatism, Ism-ism-ism')[312] and unite for peace: 'In my secret heart I wanted to write something that would take over "We Shall Overcome".'[313] Rather doubtfully, Pete ('We Shall Overcome') Seeger himself tried John's song out later that year, at the Vietnam Moratorium Day demonstration in Washington, D C, and almost 500,000 people joined in. John watched it on television, overwhelmed to see 'all those people singing it, forever and not stopping. It was one of the biggest moments of my life.'[314] But Richard Nixon, for one, would not be moved.

In July the Beatles were all back in the studio at Abbey Road to complete yet another album, which they had been recording in a desultory fashion since February. John was late turning up, as he and Yoko had needed stitches in hospital after John had run their car off the road during a nostalgic trip with Julian and Kyoko to Scotland, where they had visited his aunt Mater. In contrast to the confusion surrounding the still unreleased 'Let It Be', this new album, simply called 'Abbey Road', was being strictly controlled by George Martin and Paul McCartney. Earlier in the year John had recorded 'I Want You (She's So Heavy)', a grindingly repetitive (or subtly reiterative) minimalist tribute to Yoko, and now he produced the song that opens side one, 'Come Together'. This began as a campaign song for Timothy Leary (whose political slogan was 'Come together, join the party'),[315] but it ended up as a blues-based meditation in the surreal. John set the tone by taking his opening lines, 'Here come old flat-top, He come groovin' up slowly', from Chuck Berry's 'You Can't Catch Me' – Berry's publisher would in due course sue. With lyrics that are made all the odder by lacking normal verb inflections, 'Come Together' is so obscurely coded that many conflicting interpretations have been suggested, but in reality its message sounds loud and clear: 'One thing I can tell you is you got to be free.'[316] Disturbingly, on this last great song he ever wrote for the Beatles, John's opening words were 'Shoot me'. (The words are more audible on Take 1, which appears on 'Anthology 3', than on the finished album.)[317]

The second side of 'Abbey Road' would be one of Paul's finest hours. It opens with George's 'Here Comes The Sun'. Then John's exquisite exercise in harmony, 'Because', leads into a 16-minute medley, sculpted by Paul from a dozen or so undeveloped Lennon or McCartney song fragments. Whether they knew it or not, this was the Beatles' musical farewell. Its bittersweet climax, 'The End', for the first time ever featured solos from all four (John's characteristically growling guitar last of all), immediately followed by Paul's celebrated (if slightly vacuous) lines, 'And in the end, the love you take Is equal to the love you make.'[318]

Musically, the year was the most productive of John Lennon's life: by the end of 1969 he would have made two albums with the Beatles and released two avant-garde albums with Yoko, as well as two singles and an album with the Plastic Ono Band. That album, 'Live Peace In Toronto 1969', was recorded on 13 September at the 'Rock 'n' Roll Revival Concert', where John fronted a hastily-convened band consisting of Klaus Voorman, Eric Clapton, Alan White on drums, and Yoko. The Canadian concert was John's first conventional appearance for years, and he was literally sick with apprehension beforehand. His nervousness was excusable: Little Richard, Bo Diddley, Gene Vincent and Chuck Berry were also on the bill. 'When I hear good rock, the calibre of Chuck Berry, I just fall apart,' John once said.[319] But he did not fall apart this time, belting out the rock 'n' roll classics, 'Blue Suede Shoes', 'Money' and 'Dizzy Miss Lizzy', to start the set, while a weeping Gene Vincent watched from the wings. The band continued with three of John's own compositions (though he forgot most of the words to

'Give Peace A Chance'). Yoko finally took centre stage for her own 'Don't Worry Kyoko (Mummy's Only Looking For A Hand In The Snow)' and the 12-minute 'John John (Let's Hope For Peace)', while the guitar talents of Lennon, Clapton and Voorman supplied a background of feedback for her ululations. After the ordeal was finally over, John was buttonholed by Gene Vincent: 'Backstage he came up to me and whispered: "John, remember Hamburg? Remember all that scene?"'[320] A month later he would be dead.

Thanks to Yoko, John was now able to see himself as a 'fine artist' at last, something to which he had never aspired, even in Art College. Throughout the year he threw himself into project after project. Far from the glossy artifice of the second side of 'Abbey Road', which he would always dislike, his new art was going to be fresh, raw, unadorned and above all, personal: currently, sex was a particular preoccupation. He took up lithography, first producing a limited edition nonsense alphabet ('A is for Parrot which we can plainly see . . . F is for Ethel who lives next door . . . R is for intestines which hurt when we dance,' etc),[321] and then a suite of explicit drawings of himself and Yoko making love in various positions – at the exhibition some of these would be seized by the London police, who commented, 'Many toilet walls depict works of similar merit. It is perhaps charitable to suggest that they are the work of a sick mind.'[322] John also contributed a scene to Kenneth Tynan's controversial sex revue, *Oh Calcutta*, inspired by his teenage experiences with Pete Shotton, when during group wanks they used to put each other off by yelling out the names of particularly passion-killing celebrities – the most effective being 'Winston Churchill'.[323] In the show's programme, John's CV read: 'Born 1940. Lived. Met Yoko 1966!'[324]

With Yoko he made several further films too: it was an activity they could share as equals. *Self Portrait* was a 42-minute slow motion movie starring his own penis not quite becoming erect: 'No movement, but it dribbled at the end,'

172

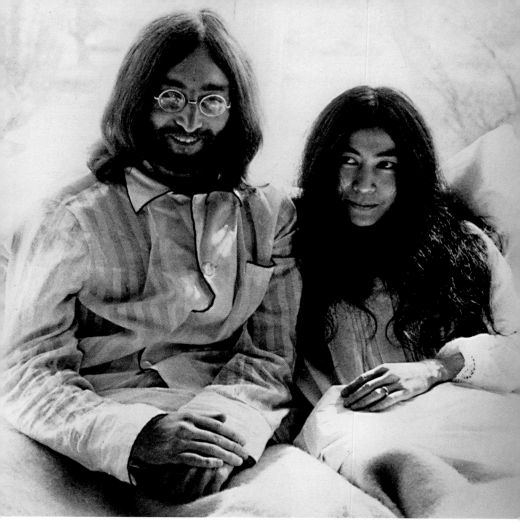

Still in bed

he later dryly commented. 'That was accidental.'[325] There would be no published reviews of this film: 'The critics wouldn't touch it,' said Yoko.[326] Possibly more uplifting was *Apotheosis*, an effective piece of what might be called ambient cinema. For this, the cameraman was instructed to film from a helium balloon while it rose over Hampshire, showing John and Yoko below, slowly shrinking into invisibility. Two distant gunshots are heard. The picture goes almost blank as the balloon enters a thick white cloud, and for some seven minutes little more than the sound of the wind interferes with the purity of the experience. Then, suddenly, the camera breaks through the strange cloud-top landscape, blue sky fills the screen, and the sun appears in glory to bring the film to a triumphant close.

While all this was going on, John and Yoko were still faced with their heroin problem. Reports of its role in his life vary considerably, and it is difficult to be certain of the extent and duration of the habit, but his statement that sniffed rather than injected the drug seems to be true. The stereotypical junkie is portrayed as a sick, desperate, lying thief, but these symptoms are largely the effect of the poverty and infection that street heroin use frequently often brings in its wake. In fact, if the supply is clean and dependable, it is possible to maintain an addiction to heroin while living a relatively healthy and active life, and this seems to have been the case with John and Yoko at around this time. John later claimed they used it as an emotional anaesthetic, taking it 'when we were in real pain. We got such a hard time from everyone.'[327]

At the end of October, the Plastic Ono Band (John, Clapton, Voorman, with Ringo on drums) released a single called 'Cold Turkey' – the title is slang for quitting heroin without medical help. That the song was informed by personal experience was at the time neither admitted by John nor generally realised by the public. In short phrases ('Rolling in pain'; 'Goosepimple bone'; 'I'll promise you anything'; 'Leave me alone', etc)[328] John recreated the physical and mental experience, ending the song with almost two minutes of terrible crying and screaming over the same grungy guitar riff, repeated over and over and over again. But if John indeed went through this appalling method of kicking the habit, it would not be very long before the drug reappeared in his life again.

John had told everyone on the plane to the Toronto concert that he was no longer a Beatle. Because 'Abbey Road' and 'Let It Be' were still to be released, he was persuaded by Allen Klein (who was currently in charge of the Beatles' finances) not to make the decision public yet.

But from now on there would be the sense of an ending about everything the Beatles did. The last time all four were together in the studio was on 20 August, when John mentioned to a shocked Paul that he was leaving the band. Two days later the final group photo session was held in the beautiful 70-acre gardens around John and Yoko's new stately home, Tittenhurst Park, in Sunningdale, near Ascot. When 'Abbey Road' was released in September, John did the usual promotional pieces for radio, but his mind was on other things.

The endless stream of interviewers to John and Yoko's office at Apple, which had become the centre of their operations, now heard about little but peace. John was finding that it was not all that simple a message to convey. Peace protestors in both Britain and America were becoming increasingly militant, and confrontations with the authorities had already led to injuries and even deaths. John wrote a letter asking the philosopher and old CND campaigner Bertrand Russell for support, and telling him that the cry was now 'Kill the pigs.'[329] In November John returned his MBE to the Queen 'in protest against Britain's involvement in the Nigeria-Biafra thing, against our support of America in Vietnam, and against "Cold Turkey" slipping down the charts.'[330] The 'Cold Turkey' joke, thrown in to lighten the tone, was unwise: it became the focus for a storm of ridicule in the newspapers, but at least Bertrand Russell wrote encouragingly: 'Whatever abuse you have suffered in the press as a result of this, I am confident that your remarks will have caused a very large number of people to think again about these wars.'[331] Aunt Mimi, however, was furious at what she called the insult to the Queen. John hadn't told her why he had wanted her to give him the medal back.

As 1969 gave way to 1970 John and Yoko fired a few more scattered shots in the battle for peace and justice. They led street protests for the cause of James Hanratty, executed for murder in 1962 after a clear miscarriage of justice. George Harrison, Keith Moon, Eric Clapton and

Billy Preston were drafted into the Plastic Ono Band for a London concert in aid of UNICEF, entitled 'Peace For Christmas'. In Canada again, during an audience with the Prime Minister, Pierre Trudeau, John secured his outline support for a great peace concert to be held there in the summer. And as a greeting to the world, a dozen cities around the globe blossomed with huge billboards and posters large and small, bearing the words 'WAR IS OVER! If You Want It. Happy Christmas from John & Yoko'. These were replaced after Christmas by others reading 'We Want It'.[332] The London *Times* bellyached about the 'unfortunate image of hippy earnestness directing liberal causes from the deep upholstery of a Beatle income'.[333] On Christmas Eve the couple fasted for peace outside Rochester Cathedral.

When the New Year arrived the couple declared that they were renaming it 'Year One A P' (for 'After Peace'),[334] and during a stay in Denmark announced that all money earned from John's records or songs would in future go to support world peace. (The idea would quickly be forgotten.) Two weeks later John and Yoko had all their hair shaved off. They gave it to be auctioned on behalf of a multiracial cultural centre in London run by the radical black organiser, Michael X. (In 1975, Michael X would be hanged in Trinidad for murder. John, convinced that the sentence was a set-up, had lobbied vainly for a pardon.) When 96 anti-apartheid protestors disrupted a Scotland-South Africa rugby match in Aberdeen, John paid £1,344 to cover all their fines.

John wrote 'Instant Karma' on 27 January. That same night the Plastic Ono Band was gathered to record it, and Phil Spector, who was in town after an invitation from John and George to see if he could do anything with the 'Let It Be' tapes, gave it his 'wall of sound' treatment. 'I wrote it for breakfast, recorded it for lunch,' said John, 'and we're putting it out for dinner.'[335] 'Instant Karma' was a call for everyone to recognise their own worth, to embrace all life has to offer, asking 'Why in the world are we here? Surely not to live in pain and fear?' Life may be short, but in the words of the anthemic chorus, 'We all shine

Michael X giving John and Yoko a pair of Muhammed Ali's bloodstained shorts in exchange for their hair

on, like the moon and the stars and the sun.'[336] John was proud of the song's simplicity: 'The greatest artists always come round to simplicity,' he said, 'I hope to record and write songs like an adult child.'[337] When it was released in Britain ten days later, it became the Plastic Ono Band's

John and Yoko and a symbolic 'Exit' sign. The photo on the left was used on the sleeve of 'Two Virgins'. The third figure is thought to be the unfortunate photographer

biggest success yet. He promised to do other 'instant' songs: 'I want records to be more like newspapers. I'd like them to come out at least once a week.'[338] But there was to be no new music from John Lennon until the following December. Something happened, or failed to happen, that suddenly stopped them in their tracks.

Fifteen years before Bob Geldof's 'Live Aid', John had realized that celebrities in the rock world might be harnessed as a force for good. He announced that he would do all he could to persuade the other Beatles to appear at the Canadian Peace Concert he had discussed with Trudeau. He would even try to get Elvis Presley. Without relinquishing ultimate control of the concert, he passed the detailed planning of the three-day event into other hands, and things seemed to be going ahead reasonably well. Then John, who had originally said that participants ought to be paid a professional fee, suddenly contradicted himself by announcing that it should be a free concert, and the whole project immediately collapsed in acrimony. To both John and Yoko, it was a devastating blow. (It would be two years before anything similar was attempted – George's 'Concert for Bangla Desh'; that too would run into hideous financial difficulties.)

After an extraordinary two years of activity and activism together, the couple seemed just to give up. John's new career as a peacenik had stalled, and the Beatles were obviously as good as dead. They retreated to their country mansion. Neither of them was happy. John didn't want to do anything except smoke dope, watch television and read. It was a state that he had spoken about to Hunter Davies in 1968: 'If I am on my own for three days, doing nothing, I almost leave myself completely. . . . I can see my hands and realize they're moving, but it's a robot who'd doing it. . . . It's frightening really, when it gets too bad. I have to see [the other Beatles] to establish contact with myself again and come down.'[339] Now if he spoke to the others, there was liable to be an argument. He didn't even want to talk to Yoko either these days. She too was miserable, and missed her daughter desperately – in January, Kyoko had been ill and they had seen a good deal of her while on a visit to Denmark, where they had stayed with her father, Tony Cox. As the Lennons hid themselves away in Tittenhurst, sniping at each other and brooding, it seemed possible that their relationship had run its course.

179

We pick our own daddy out of a dog pound of daddies[340]

You Don't Get Me Twice[341]

The irrevocable end of the Beatles, when it came on 10 April 1970, was as much a shock to themselves as it was to everyone else. Because John had agreed to say nothing after deciding to leave the band the previous September, he was a bit sore when it was Paul who suddenly made the announcement. It came as a promotional gimmick for 'McCartney', the solo album he had been quietly recording at home. Printed on the inner sleeve of the record was a series of questions and answers that spoke explicitly of his break with the Beatles for 'personal differences, business differences, musical differences'. Paul didn't know if the split would be temporary or permanent, and it sounded as if he didn't much care.[342]In fact, John's remarks in the meantime had already said it all, though they had gone largely unnoticed: he had told Marshall McLuhan for CBS television in December: 'The Beatles' pattern is one that has to be scrapped. . . . The Beatles turned into a museum, so they have to be scrapped or deformed or changed.' (McLuhan: 'They're in danger of becoming good taste?') 'They passed through that. They have to be thoroughly horsewhipped.'[343] John had even casually used the phrase 'when I was a Beatle' in a November magazine interview.[344] In 1978 he would sum up his view about the end of the Fab Four: 'I started the band. I disbanded it. It's as simple as that.'[345]

When 'Let It Be' at last came out in a black-edged box on 8 May it felt like a memorial. Paul was incensed when he discovered what Phil Spector had done, with John's connivance, to four of the tracks. He was particularly hurt when he heard 'The Long And Winding Road', potentially one of his best songs: rather than being rerecorded, John's sloppy bass playing had been drowned out by strings and a sickly female choir, the first ever heard on a Beatles record.[346] Despite these additions, Spector had cosmetically retained a sense that the album was live by salting it with irreverent remarks by John. It was perhaps insensitive to introduce Paul's most inspirational and deeply felt ballad, 'Let It Be', with the words 'And now we'd like to do *'Ark the Angels Cum,*'[347] delivered in John's broadest Scouse falsetto. John, on the other hand, thought that Spector had done a great job. He had approved of the album even before Spector's intervention, because it showed everyone: 'This is what we are like with our trousers off, so would you please end the game now?'[348] And the inclusion of one of his earliest songs, 'The One After 909', an unsophisticated skiffle railroad blues written for the Quarry Men, rounded off the career of John Lennon's little beat group very nicely.

Paul's list of the three causes for the Beatles' dissolution ('personal differences, business differences, musical differences') was accurate. However, without the first factor, the other two could probably have been dealt with through negotiation and compromise, and by allowing everyone enough freedom for their own solo projects. Fans tended to blame Yoko and Linda (who had married Paul the week before Yoko's wedding to John). It was not, of course, the women's fault that John and Paul had chosen them over the group, but ultimately it was because of them that the partnership, the rivalry, the interdependence, the old love between them had drained away. Years later, thinking back to the split, John and Paul would both separately recall the same song, a song that, as Paul said, 'we used to love in the past . . . the

184

idea that you'd been army buddies, but one day you have to kiss the army goodbye, go and get married and act like normal people.' More simply, John said: 'The old gang of mine was over the moment I met Yoko.'[349] They had both gone back in memory to those very earliest days together, two of them standing in Julia's bathroom with their cheap guitars, while she showed them the banjo chords for 'Wedding Bells (Are Breaking Up That Old Gang Of Mine)'.[350]

John's mother, and his father too, were currently very much on his mind. In March someone had sent him Arthur Janov's book, *The Primal Scream – Primal Therapy: The Cure of Neurosis*, and he had been fascinated by this method of psychotherapy, which involved revisiting and reacting to childhood traumas. For John, tortured by memories of the past that were often at odds with what Mimi and others had told him, this was an opportunity to explore who he really was, and at the same time it offered a way out of the cycle of idleness and uneasy truce with Yoko that had taken hold at Tittenhurst. Yoko too wanted to banish some of her own demons, so they summoned Janov to Britain. He found John in 'about as much pain as I've ever seen in my life',[351] and told the couple that if they wanted him to help them, all they had to do was to give up drink, tobacco, alcohol, recreational drugs, television, radio and the telephone, and (for the first time in two years) stay away from each other. On April Fool's day John and Yoko issued a press release to announce that they were undergoing dual sex-change operations, and offered themselves up for an introductory month of 'primal' at his London clinic.

Janov's methods were not endorsed by the psychiatric establishment. He encouraged his patients to express their long-buried agonies by cathartic screaming and crying. Every day John was helped to discover 'the little child inside the man' (as he would sing a decade later).[352] He was 'regressed' to the age at which, so Janov maintained, most adult problems begin, between about four and seven, when children are forming their first links to a world no longer mediated through parental love. These were the years during which John had been fought over by Julia, Freddie and Mimi, a time of puzzling rejections and nameless fears. In the course of treatment, he suddenly remembered playing on a beach somewhere (in fact Blackpool), while a long way off behind him his father was chatting to a friend. Without warning, the ground had somehow opened beneath him and swallowed him up, leaving him trapped at the bottom of a large pit in the sand, screaming in panic. It felt like hours before his father finally bestirred himself to look for him. For John, the incident seemed to sum everything up. For the first time he recognized that he had been grossly neglected as a boy, not only by his father but, almost unthinkably, by his mother as well. 'In the therapy you really feel every painful moment of your life,' he would explain later. 'It's excruciating. You are forced to realize your own pain, the kind that makes you wake up afraid with your heart pounding.'[353]

Leaving Paul to get on with his own breakdown in the middle of negotiations about the winding up of the group – he was at loggerheads with the others about the appointment of Allen Klein as business manager – John and Yoko flew to their psychotherapist's Los Angeles headquarters for four more months of intensive therapy. They would eventually withdraw in high dudgeon at the end of August after Yoko fell out with Janov, who had apparently started tackling John's seemingly helpless dependence upon her. But by then John had got what he wanted from the course, and as a bonus it had unlocked a rich creative seam that was producing many new songs. In subsequent interviews, his evaluation of Janov was unusually down-to-earth: 'Primal Therapy allowed us to feel feelings continually, and those feelings usually make you cry. That's all.'[354] That the treatment was simple did not mean, however, that it had not changed his life: 'It was the most important thing that happened to me

Yoko and John, with Julian on his lap, between Eric Clapton (left) and Brian Jones at the 'Rock 'n' Roll Circus'

besides meeting Yoko and being born.'[355]

By the end of September, John was back in the studio, urgently recording an album. The past months had clarified a great deal in his mind. He was still an angry man, but for the first time in his life he knew what he was angry about. A great part of it had to do with children.

187

He could now understand how his parents, both of them, had damaged him. He also knew that he had probably already done much the same thing to his own son, and that there was nothing practical he could do about that now – the last time he had gone to see Julian and Cynthia at Janov's suggestion, Yoko had phoned in the throes of a threatening emotional crisis and demanded that he come home at once. He might perhaps have cared for Kyoko but she was kept well out of reach by her father. And Yoko had suffered two more miscarriages in the last year: it seemed blindingly obvious that they were never going to have a child together – probably something to do with all the drugs he had taken over the years.

At this point, Freddie Lennon, who had contacted John mentioning that he was about to write his autobiography, was invited to Tittenhurst for his 30th birthday on 9 October 1970. They hadn't met for almost three years. With his young wife Pauline and their 18-month-old son David, John's new half-brother, he arrived in time for lunch, bearing a gift-wrapped bottle of aftershave for the currently bearded ex-Beatle. According to Pauline Lennon, who wrote the only published eyewitness account of what then took place, John immediately went on the attack. Appearing to be very stoned on some drug, he told his father to get off his back; he was cutting off his allowance at once and evicting them from the house he had given them in Brighton. At the top of his voice he yelled at Freddie: 'Have you any idea what I've been through because of you? Day after day in therapy, screaming for my daddy, sobbing for you to come home.' He began obscenely abusing Julia as well: his mother had been nothing but a whore. 'Look at me! I'm bloody mad, insane,' he shouted. 'I'm due for an early death like Hendrix or Joplin, and it's all your fault. Do you know what it does to a child to be asked to choose between his parents? You call yourself a father? You think that screwing some woman gives you the right to call yourself a father?' John pointed at little David,

188

now clinging onto Pauline's legs. 'Lock him away from his parents and ordinary human beings and see how he'll end up – he'll end up a raving lunatic just like me.'

As John's birthday visitors made for the door, he seized his father by the lapels and hissed into his face: 'As for your life story, you're never to write *anything* without my approval, and if you tell anyone what happened here today . . . I'll have you killed. I'll have you cased up in a box and dumped out at sea right in the middle of the ocean . . .'[356] Freddie Lennon, the old sailor who could not swim, turned and ran. He would be too frightened ever to get in contact with his son again.

That evening, John was heard singing to himself, 'Happy birthday to me, happy birthday to me!'[357] He was in the studio with Ringo and Klaus, trying to record a new number called 'Remember', a bitter and charmless meditation on parents – your 'Ma and Pa', it said, were never the ones who had to suffer when you were little. John made at least four attempts to get through the song. One of them appears on the 1998 'Lennon Anthology', a four-cd collection of live or unfinished music, where John sounds as if he can hardly stand, interrupting himself frequently with half-hysterical giggles. As the music begins, he says 'This is a story about . . . This is a story . . .' and then gives up the struggle and starts to sing: 'Well, remember when you were young, How the hero was never hung, Always got away? And remember how the man Used to leave you empty-handed, Always, always let you down?' After muddling and repeating words in the chorus ('And don't you worry About what you've done, And don't feel sorry About what's been said and done'),[358] John calls a halt, and so never reaches the lines that on the finished version will lead the song towards its explosive conclusion: 'If you ever feel so sad And the whole world is driving you mad, Remember, remember today.'[359] A little while later, George Harrison popped in with a present, a special recording of 'It's Johnny's Birthday' which he had made secretly with Ringo.

Freddie, for one, would always remember that day: the

John Lennon 1975

fallout from his son's experiences with Arthur Janov had been a terrible shock for him. Still, the treatment had been artistically liberating for John. Over the next year, he would write, record and release the two albums upon which his post-Beatles reputation would largely depend during the

1970s. The first, called simply 'John Lennon / Plastic Ono Band' came out in December 1970. Known as the 'Primal Scream Album', it was something entirely new in rock, closer to the anguished blues lamentations of the Mississippi delta than to the expertly polished products of Abbey Road Studios. Even though Phil Spector was involved in the mixing process, the sound throughout is lean to the point of emaciation. The music dispenses with technical artifice (apart from the usual distancing filters and echoes on John's vocals), allowing Ringo and Klaus to lay down a bare, solid sound picture behind his guitar or piano. John's voice dominates throughout, an instrument whose versatility was scarcely noticed during his Beatle years, sometimes swooping and tremulous, or lit with sweetness as it hovers high around a note, and sometimes an unbridled throaty scream or a moan forced out through gritted teeth.

The album opens with the tolling of a funeral bell. After four long, deep chimes, without warning a high voice calls out the word 'Mother!' and the music begins, emphatic piano chords slowly fading to nothingness over a sparse bass, driven reluctantly forward by Ringo's dulled drum tattoo. And over this dead march John is accusing her, 'you had me, but I never had you'. The second verse addresses his father similarly ('you left me, but I never left you'), and the third warns children not to follow in their parents' footsteps (as John has already done with Julian). Then, abruptly, the rhythm changes, and repeated calls of 'Momma don't go' and 'Daddy come home'[360] gradually build in intensity, until John's unrestrained howls of torment sound like a child in the grip of a hysterical tantrum. It is not easy listening.

After a comforting ballad, 'Hold On', which acts as a short and necessary break for John and Yoko to calm and reassure each other – the first of three such interludes on the album – John returns to the fray with 'I Found Out', attacking those who would like to control him, purveyors of trendy do-goodism, Christian propaganda, male chauvinism, parental neglect ('They didn't want me so they made me a star'), Indian mysticism and even drugs ('Can't do you no harm to feel your own pain').[361]

'Working Class Hero', the next track, continues the theme. It is John's most impassioned attempt to capture the essence of the genuine folk song. 'As kids we were all opposed to folk songs because they were so middle-class,' he would recall in 1971. 'I liked Dominic Behan a bit and there was some good stuff to be heard in Liverpool. Occasionally you hear very old records on the radio or TV of real workers in Ireland singing, and the power is fantastic.'[362] In this angry and much misinterpreted polemical ballad, whose message is simple: 'Think for yourself!', John turns from the false leaders of 'I Found Out' to those who have been brainwashed from childhood into becoming followers. John's 'working class hero' is the same dupe as Robert Tressell's 'ragged trousered philanthropist'. You either proudly serve the leaders who exploit you or else, 'doped with religion and sex and TV,' you allow ambition to lure you into the viciousness of the capitalist work ethic. Whichever way you choose, John sings, 'you're still fuckin' peasants as far as I can see.' The song's refrain, and its conclusion, share a bitter irony that was missed by almost everyone: 'A working class hero is something to be. If you want to be a hero well just follow me.'[363]

'God' is the climax of the album's exploration of the public and private forces that form (and deform) us all. It is John's personal *credo*, or rather *non credo*, a major statement of what he no longer believes in. One of the most quoted of his later songs, it begins with a sceptical denial of any autonomous supreme being: 'God is a concept by which we measure our pain,' and then goes on to dismiss all John's old heroes one by one, the last, definitively, being 'I don't believe in Beatles'. After a pause to allow this to sink in, he sings, 'I just believe in me, Yoko and me. That's reality.' The song ends by handing over to his

192

listeners: 'And so dear friends, You just have to carry on. The dream is over.'[364]

'John Lennon/Plastic Ono Band' may in time be remembered as his greatest single work: 'I think it's "Sgt Lennon",' he said in interview after it was released. 'I don't really know how it will sink in, where it will lie, in the spectrum of rock 'n' roll and the generation and all the rest of it, but I know what it is. It's something else, it's another door. . . . In one way it's terribly uncommercial, it's so miserable in a way and heavy; but it's reality, and I'm not going to veer away from it for anything.'[365] The final song on the album is very short and simple, a two verse coda that brings it back to where it all began, in childhood, with John's mother. But, in case we have forgotten, Julia is dead. Recorded deliberately badly on a portable tape recorder, 'My Mummy's Dead' sounds like a boy singing to himself in an empty room the day after the funeral, making up the words as he goes along. In one sense, that is what John Lennon has been doing all along.

A case could be made that, particularly after the end of the Beatles, interviews were almost as important a mode of expression for John as music. His most famous one, a long dialogue with Jann Wenner, was published in two parts in *Rolling Stone* at the beginning of 1971. It was the first time anyone had spoken so candidly about certain sensitive matters, such as the drugs and debauchery of the moptop years, and it would be an invaluable source of information on many aspects of his life and career. However, since John was in an exceptionally touchy and belligerent frame of mind, he was frequently misleading in both tone and content, and contrived to be very rude about almost everyone he mentioned (except for Yoko, who sat beside him throughout.) His remarks would be resented for years to come by many old comrades and members of his family. Paul and George, though not Ringo, got tongue-lashings, but they found it a little easier to deal with. As John said, 'They don't care, they've been with me for 15 or 20 years, they know damn well what I'm like.' Later, when the interview came out in book form without his permission (as *Lennon Remembers*), John was angry, since it would now reach people (such as Aunt Mimi) who might otherwise not have seen it. 'I don't really like hurting people, but Jann Wenner questioned me when I was almost still in therapy and you can't play games. You're opened up. It was like he got me on an acid trip. Things come out.'[366]

John's most popular solo album, 'Imagine', topped the charts on both sides of the Atlantic in the autumn of 1971. John referred to it as being like the previous one but 'with sugar coating'.[367] He included gentle songs like 'Jealous Guy', 'Oh Yoko' and the title track, as well as the paradoxically jolly barrelhouse of 'Crippled Inside' (which some said was directed at Paul McCartney). But there were other numbers in which the uncompromising edge of his previous album was evident, such as 'Gimmie Some Truth', a glorious decantation of abusive scorn over President Nixon and his supporters ('short-haired yellow-bellied son of Tricky Dicky', 'neurotic psychotic pig-headed politicians', 'tight-lipped condescending mama's little chauvinists' and so on).[368] Likewise, 'How Do You Sleep?' showered the unfortunate Paul with pun-laden invective worthy of Ireland's angrier Gaelic bards, who would have been proud of lines like 'Those freaks was right when they said you was dead' and 'The only thing you done was yesterday'.[369] John later claimed that the bitterness of this song was largely an artistic ploy: 'I wasn't really feeling that vicious at the time, but I was using my resentment towards Paul to create a song.'[370] Cold comfort, especially as in 'Imagine' he mocked the sleeve of Paul's second album 'Ram' (where a pastoral Paul holds a sheep by the horns) with a free postcard showing himself pulling a pig's ears.

Today, the title track of 'Imagine' is so familiar, and for a time after John's death, was so poignant, that it is impossible to judge it afresh on its merits. In 1975 John dismissed the idea that it was his best album: 'As far as I'm concerned, the best piece of work I ever put out is still the 'Mother'/'Working Class Hero' album.'[371] John and Yoko both said that 'Imagine' was inspired by Yoko's *Grapefruit* recipes for life (such as 'Imagine your body spreading rapidly all over the world like a thin tissue . . .'[372]) and no doubt it was so, but it is worth noting that the pivotal, thrice repeated, line 'Imagine all the people' was first used in John's 1965 book, *A Spaniard in the Works*, in a poem called 'The Fat Budgie', about a bird who ate so much scrambled egg on toast that he was in danger of needing a crutch. The last eight lines of the poem, in retrospect, are intriguing:

> It would be funny wouldn't it
> A budgie on a stick
> Imagine all the people
> Laughing till they're sick.
>
> So that's my budgie Jeffrey
> Fat and yellow too
> I love him more than daddie
> And I'm only thirty two.[373]

John was six weeks short of his 32nd year when he and Yoko left England on 31 August 1971, between the making of 'Imagine' and its release in September. Yoko was 38. Her efforts to have Kyoko living with her before she was grown up had turned into a crusade. The previous April she and John had been arrested after tracking down the seven-year-old in Majorca: they had removed her from a playground while her father was at a meditation session (with the Maharishi, of all people). Kyoko was then asked by a judge to decide between her parents. She had chosen her father. Another judge in the Virgin Islands (where Yoko had been officially divorced from Tony Cox) had granted custody to Yoko. Believing that father and daughter were now in America, the Lennons went to New York, and booked into a hotel. John was never to see England again.

I always thought the Statue of Liberty said 'Come'[374]

Qué Pasa New York?

When he arrived in the USA, John found himself with no clear idea of what he was going to do there. 'The first people who got in touch with me was Jerry Rubin and Abbie Hoffman,' he would recall. 'And the next thing you know, I'm doin' John Sinclair benefits and one thing and another. I'm pretty movable, as an artist, you know.'[376] But it was not just the influence of those two irrepressible Yippies ('the Mork and Mindy of the Sixties', John called them[377]) that got him involved in radical protest in New York: he had been active on many fronts since 1969. On 11 August, for example, not long before leaving England, he had demonstrated outside the Ulster Office in London, telling *The Times* that his protest was twofold: to oppose internment and the use of troops in Northern Ireland, and to support the editors of *Oz*, recently imprisoned after a celebrated obscenity trial. (He had even written a single to raise money for the fight, 'God Save Us / Do The Oz'.) 'The two matters,' he said, 'are integral and cannot be divided.'[378] The next day he sent £1,000 to striking shipbuilders on the Clyde. The only important link between these causes (and many others that he embraced during these months) was in John's head: each was an engagement in his continuing battle against the establishment, its rules and its conventions. And that battle was ultimately rooted in John Lennon's sense of what it was to be an artist, and what it was to be free. Both, as he would one day acknowledge, involved a deep-seated internal struggle to 'avoid being normal'.[379]

It was really Tariq Ali, one of the intellectual driving forces behind Britain's New Left, who first harnessed John Lennon politically. After conversations with Ali in the spring of 1971, John wrote an anthem for use at demonstrations, 'Power To The People'. The song was now cropping up at the ever more militant Vietnam rallies in the USA. (So was 'Give Peace A Chance', though marchers were now chanting 'All we are saying is get Nixon's ass'.)[380] From earlier visits to the city John was already a familiar face at New York protests. Now he was everywhere: performing at a benefit for those shot by troopers in the Attica prison riots, singing in support of John Sinclair, who had been given ten years for the possession of cannabis (two joints), demanding civil rights for American Indians at Syracuse, and on 22 April speaking on Vietnam at the New York National Peace Rally, before leading the crowds into 'Give Peace A Chance'.

John was aware of his reputation as a Jack of all Causes. 'I'm always getting accused of hopping from subject to subject – "one minute he's on meditation, the next he's on peace,"' he told an interviewer. 'Well, the Irish thing isn't new for me. I was always on the Irish thing.'[381] In his heart, perhaps, he always had been: now, in New York, far more than he ever had in London, John felt the pull of his Irishness. He was in a similar position to the many Irish-Americans, often two or more generations away from Ireland, who still valued their ancestral roots. After 'Bloody Sunday', 30 January 1971, when 13 Catholics were shot in Northern Ireland by British troops during civil rights unrest, he started to do something more about it. At a protest outside the New York offices of BOAC to show 'sympathy for the 13 people who were mercilessly shot down by the British imperialists'[382] (as John put it in his best agit-speak), he sang with Yoko a recent song, 'The Luck Of The Irish'. Unfortunately, to native Irish ears at least, this would-be republican ballad was humiliatingly simplistic, with lines like 'If you could drink dreams like Irish streams

200

Then the world would be high as the mountains of morn' (sic). It endorsed two equally untenable myths, that 'British brigands' were currently committing 'genocide' in Northern Ireland, and that the island was teeming with leprechauns, shamrocks and rainbows capable of bearing your weight. The song's single autobiographical verse at least explained where John's sympathies with the old country had begun:

> In the 'Pool they told us the story,
> How the English divided the land,
> Of the pain and the death and the glory,
> And the poets of old Ireland.[383]

After the 'Bloody Sunday' protest in New York on 5 February 1972 John drafted a press release: 'Representatives of the IRA spoke, including some secret leaders who had flown in especially for the meeting, considering its importance to try to awaken the American Irish who are rather middle-class. . . . Before John and Yoko sang, Lennon made a short speech about his Irish ancestry, and the main thing he said was "My name is Lennon and you can guess the rest," which got a great round of applause from the people. And he stressed the fact of his Liverpool upbringing, an area 80 per cent dominated by Irish descent.'[384]

If Freddie Lennon saw the report on the front page of *The Times* the next day, he might have been proud. John quickly wrote a marginally better 'newspaper' song called 'Sunday Bloody Sunday', couched more confidently in the Irish rebel ballad tradition. It was a crudely sentimental polemic of the sort that in the late 1950s was commonplace in the pubs of Liverpool, and was until recently still heard in Irish-American republican circles:

> Well it was Sunday Bloody Sunday
> When they shot the people there.
> The cries of thirteen martyrs
> Filled the Free Derry air.
> Is there anyone amongst you
> Dare to blame it on the kids?
> Not a soldier boy was bleeding
> When they nailed the coffin lids![385]

201

By now, the FBI had built up a thick dossier about John Lennon, detailing any of his activities or statements that could be construed as subversive, and charting their efforts to have him deported as a revolutionary (though his 1968 drug conviction was always used as the official excuse). The Bureau reported progress to the President's chief of staff, H R Haldeman – and so presumably it reached Richard Nixon himself as well. Meanwhile, John spoke frequently to radio and television audiences (notably on the chatshows of Dick Cavett and Mike Douglas), complaining of official harassment – his phone was being tapped, and he was being openly followed by the CIA. The real reason the Immigration and Naturalization Service was trying to expel him, he said, was nothing to do with cannabis; it was because he was a peacenik –an accusation that would eventually be confirmed by released FBI and other documents. 'I was half hoping I could bend spoons on *The Mike Douglas Show*,' he would write later. 'But I settled for bending a few minds.'[386] (In 1975 he recalled that the day after he mentioned the surveillance on TV, it stopped.)

Paradoxically, because the authorities wanted rid of him, John was effectively trapped in the USA: if he ever left the country, it was unlikely that he would have been allowed back. Having initially gained entry on a nine-month visa, such tenure as he had was stressfully uncertain, as it depended on repeated brief stays of execution, each of which had to be argued through the courts. It would be July 1976 before John finally got his green card, by which time many influential figures would have made statements on his behalf, including Fred Astaire, Norman Mailer, both the Mayor and the Bishop of New York, and even Gloria Swanson, whom he had met in a healthfood store. The judge at the hearing would say, 'Lennon's four-year battle to remain in our country is testimony to his faith in the American dream.'[387]

December 1971 had seen the release of the jolly 'Happy Xmas (War is Over)' in the USA. Though it was not an immediate hit, it would become a seasonal standard in years to come. But it could not be denied that John's musical output now lacked direction, or passion, or as he might have put it, pain. After the success of 'Imagine', John had said 'Now I understand what you have to do: put your political message across with a little honey.'[388] However, when his double album, 'Some Time in New York City', was released on 12 June 1972, there was no honey on it at all. The verdict of public and critic alike was damning: the first disc (recorded with a New York bar-room band called Elephant's Memory) was largely a laborious collection of off-the-peg agitprop protest songs – including his Irish ballads; the second was a disposable ragbag of live performances, on which Yoko's free-form vocals figured prominently. Though the song, 'New York City', was fun, with a lyric describing John and Yoko's recent experiences there ('Tried to shake our image Just a-cycling through the Village, But found that we had left it back in London . . .'),[389] only 'Woman Is The Nigger Of The World', one of the few songs worthy of the Women's Liberation Movement, would last at all. (During rehearsals for two triumphant shows in Central Park at the end of August on behalf of handicapped children, John would be heard changing the song's controversial 'N-word' to 'nipple', rather spoiling his feminist credentials.)[390]

After this, John's activism diminished rapidly, and he withdrew from high profile campaigning. He would do one more benefit appearance for the handicapped (which cynics said was an attempt to curry favour with the powerful), and then he substantially reverted to his core belief, that the personal was already the political. It was an understandable withdrawal, for several reasons. John was becoming nervous about who his enemies were and what they might do to him: after the Watergate break-in in June 1972, rumours of 'dirty tricks' were everywhere. How far would Nixon go to silence his opponents? His 'journalism' album had been a flop; and it hadn't changed anything either, as far as he could see. Furthermore, he had urgent matters to deal with in his own life. Having kicked heroin, he and Yoko now had the more difficult job of getting off methadone (a prescription drug used to wean addicts off heroin.) In the summer of 1972 they took a course of acupuncture, then illegal in America, and managed to get clean. The therapist also gave Yoko a potion to increase her fertility, but to no avail. After more searching for Kyoko, and even some fruitless negotiating with Tony Cox, some months later Yoko was again awarded custody of Kyoko, this time by a judge on the American mainland, but by then father and daughter had disappeared completely. Tensions between the Lennons, childless and artistically jaded, were mounting.

On the night in November 1972 when Nixon was swept back into the White House for a second term, John was feral in his anger, humiliating Yoko at a party by going off to a bedroom with another woman. Thereafter, he went musically quiet for over a year, spending most of it watching television in their flat in Greenwich Village. He wasn't entirely idle, though: he helped Yoko to record a feminist double album with Elephant's Memory in the autumn and wrote a song ('I'm The Greatest') for Ringo in the spring. In June he was seen with Yoko at the Watergate hearings in Washington, taking in a quick demonstration at the South Vietnamese embassy on the way home. In September he reviewed a book of Goon Show scripts for the *New York Times*. (In his youth their humour had been 'a conspiracy against reality,' he wrote, 'the only proof that the WORLD was insane.')[391]

At long last, after the couple had moved to a large apartment in the balefully gothic Dakota Building overlooking Central Park, John dug up some songs and bits of songs that he had floating around, fiddled around with them and, chiefly to fulfil the terms of a contract, recorded an album called 'Mind Games'. Though the result was nothing to be ashamed of, it broke no new ground. 'The only reason I make albums is because you're supposed to. It's rock 'n' roll at different speeds,' he said helpfully during a promotional interview. 'There's no very deep message about it.'[392] The record was released in November 1973, and reached number nine on both sides of the Atlantic, but the truth was that 'Mind Games' did not make for particularly enjoyable or interesting listening. It was eclipsed by new albums from

Paul and even Ringo, both coincidentally issued the same month: 'Ringo' reached number two in the US and six in the UK, while 'Band On The Run' would sell six million copies worldwide by the end of 1974.

With its blend of apology, self-justification and anger, 'Mind Games' was disturbingly eloquent about the state of John's relationship with Yoko. Both titles and lyrics often sounded like stages in an argument that he was losing, typical examples being: 'I know and I'm guilty (yes I am) But I never could read your mind' in 'I Know (I Know)'[393] or, oddly phrased in the continuous present, 'And when I hurt you and cause you pain, Darlin' I promise I won't do it again' in 'Aisumasen (I'm Sorry)'.[394] Precisely what was going on between the Lennons at this time is anyone's guess. Sexually, it would seem, very little. During the second half of 1973, perhaps adopting the Japanese tradition of the geisha as a release valve for a stale marriage, Yoko encouraged John to begin a physical relationship with May Pang, the Lennon's 22-year-old secretary. Then in October, while Yoko was away at a feminist conference in Chicago, John suddenly ran off with May to Los Angeles. It was the beginning of his so-called 'Lost Weekend', and it would last for 16 months.

Generally explained as a premature mid-life crisis, John's time in LA was more like a belated sowing of youthful wild oats. He had married young, and for all the debauchery of the Beatles' world tours, he had missed that enjoyable rite of passage which many men experience in their twenties, just hanging out with mates and getting drunk, with no real responsibilities. But there were differences. Later, John would say 'It's all right wondering whether the grass is greener on the other side, but once you get there, all you find is more grass.'[395] John's mates were not carefree young men, and it wasn't only grass they found in Los Angeles. Most of John's circle there were in similar situations to his, famous married musicians who had left home, bringing their drink or drug problems with them. There were the Who's legendary drummer Keith Moon, never a model of good behaviour,

Harry Nilsson (on a non-stop bender), Ringo (currently on one) and the brilliant, if drug-riddled, guitarist Jesse Ed Davis, who became a particular friend. Even the Beatles' dear old roadie, Mal Evans, was there, drunk, stoned and maudlin about the old days. Amid the clouds of smoke there was acid, smack, cocaine on tap and anything else you thought you might like to try. But perhaps worst of all was when Ringo turned everybody on to brandy alexanders – essentially a lethally alcoholic type of milk shake.

Phil Spector, rarely a calming influence, was also in LA, and soon they were in the studio together, trying to record an album of John's favourite rock 'n' roll songs, the ones that had made him a musician in the first place. It was a good idea, but the atmosphere in the studio was tense and undisciplined. 'We both ended up drinking,' said John later. 'So, I don't know, it just got into a big madhouse.'[396] Spector was jagged with paranoia, even at one point shooting bullets into the ceiling. 'Phil,' John said, 'if you're going to kill me, kill me. But don't fuck with my ears. I need 'em.'[397] Though dozens of musicians were hired ('40 guys all playing out of tune'), very little usable material resulted. Later, back in New York, but still not reconciled with Yoko, John would try again, and in 1975 February an album was finally to appear, called simply 'Rock 'n' Roll', made up of the best of the LA sessions and some newly recorded tracks. 'It was the worst time of my life, that record,' John would say. 'I don't think many people really listened to it without seeing a guy with a Tampax on his head. . . . If I forget about the way it was made and just hear it, it ain't so bad.'[398] Nor is it, with songs on it that meant as much to John as 'Be Bop A Lula' and 'Bony Maronie' (which he remembered singing 'the only time my mother saw me perform before she died.')[399] However, even today the record is diminished by the sense of how much better it could have been.

John was photographed, fighting drunk, outside a Hollywood night-club. Stories of some his 'Lost Weekend' excesses (such as the 'sanitary towel incident') were now appearing in the gossip magazines, and there were even

John, May Pang, Harry Nilsson and some brandy alexanders in Los Angeles

worse episodes that were hushed up. 'It was such a mess that I can hardly remember what happened. I was away from Yoko and I wanted to come back. . . . When I was still drunk I would just ramble on or scream abuse at her or beg her to come back, between Dr Jekyll and Mr Hyde.'[400] Despite the attentions of May Pang (by now well coached in the esoterica of John's sexual predilections), he oscillated between depression and rage, both of which had always been exacerbated by drink. 'I get my daily Yoko out of a bottle these days,' he said.[401] Then in early 1974, while sharing a beach house at Santa Monica with his rat-pack of rat-arsed friends, John began tiring of the madness. He hosted a couple of Sunday night jam sessions with passing musicians, including Paul McCartney (it was the last time they were ever caught on tape or camera together), and he produced an album, 'Pussycats', for a deteriorating Harry Nilsson. Then, at the end of April, he left them all and went back to New York to finish mixing it.

By June John and May were living together in a pleasant apartment on Sutton Place, and things were returning to an even keel. He began to pick up with old mates such as Mick Jagger, and saw Paul once more for a couple of days, enjoyably talking over old times. He also began phoning Mimi again, whom he had been neglecting. Julian, now almost a teenager, flew to New York in July, and played drums on a song ('Ya Ya') that they recorded together. Over the next months John would contact other members of the clan as well. 'I've been wanting a family,' he told his half-sister Julia, 'and I've had one all along.'[402]

With a basic group including Klaus Voorman, Jesse Ed Davis, Nicky Hopkins and Jim Keltner, John prepared a new album, 'Walls and Bridges', which was released at the end of September. The title was, he felt, 'sort of poetic, and it says everything without saying anything.'[403] John's renewed interest in his roots was echoed on the album sleeve and accompanying booklet of lyrics, which reproduced eight of his schoolboy paintings, and included information about the Lennon family, lifted in facsimile from a book about Irish families. The piece ended with the assertion: 'no person of this name has distinguished himself in the political, military or cultural life of Ireland, or for that matter in England either.' Below this statement, in John's handwriting, appear the words, 'Oh yeah?'

John wrote that 'Walls and Bridges' was 'an unconcept album.'[404] He would later dismiss the material as 'craftsmanship writing'.[405] But there was good stuff on it, better than anything since the days of 'Imagine', and the

With Elton John on stage at Madison Square Garden, November 1974

musicianship was impeccable. Ambiguously, John included May Pang in his love songs for Yoko, and in a biting attack ('Steel and Glass') on Allen Klein, the Beatles' negotiator *extraordinaire* (who was now out of favour), he accused himself as well. There were several songs from his 'Lost Weekend', notably 'Whatever Gets You Thru The Night', with Elton John on piano, and the final track on the album, 'Nobody Loves You When You're Down And Out'. This last, a beautifully modulated and bitter cry from the depths, was one of John Lennon's last great songs, revealing the hollow reality behind stardom: 'But still you ask me do I love you . . . All I can tell you is it's all show biz.' It ends with the prescient line: 'Everybody loves you when you're six foot in the ground.'[406]

At the beginning of February 1975, John went back to his life with Yoko in the Dakota. In interviews, they would romantically insist that the reconciliation had begun over two months earlier, on 28 November, when after Elton John's concert at Madison Square Garden they had a backstage 'moment of silence.'[407] (John had promised Elton to appear with him if 'Whatever Gets You Thru The Night' made number one in the US singles charts, which it most surprisingly did – in the UK it reached only number 24.) John's short set finished with 'I Saw Her Standing There', written, as he announced, 'by an old estranged fiancé of mine called Paul.'[408] The song had been the first track on the Beatles' first album; now it would turn out to be John's last ever live public performance. Even without Yoko, it would have been an emotional night: 'it meant a lot to me and it meant a hell of a lot to Elton [...], and he was in tears,' said John later. 'I felt guilty 'cause I wasn't in tears.'[409]

Before he disappeared into the Dakota, there was still time for John to make one more musical excursion, this time with David Bowie, whom he had met in LA. In January 1975 he played rhythm guitar on 'Across The Universe'(a song of his own from 'Let It Be'), for inclusion in Bowie's 'Young Americans' album. Afterwards in a jam they came up with a new number together, 'Fame', which would top the charts and make Bowie's name in the USA. John summed up the session in a phrase: 'I had fun!'[410] But apart from playing piano on two songs for another of Ringo's LPs in June 1976, there were to be no similar collaborations. Indeed John was to make no further studio recordings until August 1980. He had decided, he told a friend, 'to be or not to be for a coupla years.'[411] On 6 March a press release explained to everyone that the Lennons' 'separation hadn't worked out.'[412] As

210

John and Yoko before the separation

spring bloomed over Central Park, John gave *Rolling Stone* his last substantial interview for four years: 'I feel like I've been on Sinbad's voyage, you know, and I've battled all those monsters and I've got back,' he said. He was now thinking of the long term. 'If I let the Top Ten dominate my art, then the art will die. . . . What do you want to be? What are you lookin' for?' he asked himself. 'I'm a freakin' artist, man, not a fuckin' racehorse.'[413]

Over the next few months, John would be seen and

heard less and less. In April, to promote what he called his 'Oldies but Mouldies'[414] rock 'n' roll album John did a few songs for 'Whispering' Bob Harris on BBC2's *The Old Grey Whistle Test*. Under legal duress he did some more – fronting a band called BOMF, or Brothers of Mother Fuckers – for a cheesy ITV celebration of the seemingly endless life of Sir Lew Grade, who in 1969 had grabbed control of Northern Songs. (John made the band pointedly two-faced for the occasion by giving them masks to wear on the back of their heads.) There were a few more chatty television and radio shows but then, after the couple went on holiday in June to Long Beach, that was about it.

Yoko would compare their relationship to the romantic and affectionate marriage between the Victorian poets Robert Browning and Elizabeth Barrett. On Mimi's shelves at Mendips while John was growing up there had been a much more intriguing analogy, however, and John now made the connection (though it was one whose nuances may have been missed by Yoko.) This was another famous literary pairing, the alcoholic Irish-American genius F Scott Fitzgerald, author of *The Great Gatsby* and other largely autobiographical fictions, and his disturbed wife Zelda. As iconic for the Jazz Age as John and Yoko would be for the late 1960s, the Fitzgeralds' devotion to each other was legendary. But their marriage was ravaged by tension and misery and, while Zelda went mad, her husband sank into frustrated silence, as the effects of drink, celebrity and too many late nights strangled his abilities. In a posthumous collection of scraps, Fitzgerald said of himself, 'ten years this side of forty-nine, I suddenly realised that I had prematurely cracked'.[415] John was now 35, and not unaware of the danger that a lapse into silence might be the first signs of a similar disintegration in him too. There was at least one great difference between the Lennons and the Fitzgeralds, however. Against all the odds, Yoko, at 42, was pregnant again. For the next few months, they both concentrated on keeping healthy. After the three previous failures, they would do all they could not to lose this baby. It felt like a last chance.

In the early autumn, John wrote to the onetime press officer of the Beatles, Derek Taylor, old correspondent and enthusiastic LSD partner, telling him that he was enjoying his pregnancy and felt in no hurry to do anything else at all. He was relaxing, thinking, giving himself some 'what's it all about time . . . I'll outlive the bastards in more ways than one,' he said. 'My head and body are as clear as a bell.' He did, however, mention 'some nice window pane' (LSD) as well as 'some incredibly LEGAL MUSHROOMS!'[416] Presumably, though he was treating his body with care, the retired psychic cosmonaut was still taking his mind on the occasional therapeutic day trip into inner space.

On 9 October 1975, by emergency caesarian section, Yoko gave birth to a boy in New York Hospital. As only just over eight months had elapsed since John's return to the Dakota, perhaps the child's arrival was a little premature, but he was a good weight, 6lb 10oz. 'I feel higher than the Empire State Building,' said the proud father.[417] The date was auspicious: Yoko, a recent convert to astrology, was particularly pleased that Sean Taro Ono Lennon, as their son was to be called, had been born on John's 35th birthday. Elton John was chosen as godfather. Apple celebrated the good news by releasing 'Shaved Fish', a compilation of John's greatest hits since the Beatles. It seemed to round everything off very nicely.

Just before Christmas, there was a loud hammering on the door of Apartment 72 of the Dakota, and the occupants could hear the merry sound of carols being rather tunefully sung outside. It was Paul and Linda, in town to visit Linda's parents. Nine months had passed since the lawyers had at last announced: 'All matters in the dispute between Mr McCartney and John Lennon, George Harrison and Ringo Starr have been fully settled.'[418] The statement had marked the final dissolution of The Beatles and Co partnership. John, Yoko and Sean gave their unexpected guests a warm welcome, and they all sat down for a lovely long chat.

The camel dances and having danced moves on [419]

Life in Peace[420]

And so began John Lennon's time as a 'househusband', his private years. Accounts of his activities and his state of mind during this time differ markedly. Some commentators have portrayed the ex-Beatle as a junkie again, depressed and alone, or watching television in an almost catatonic state for days on end, unaware that Yoko (also said to be back on heroin) was plotting to divorce him. Others, including Yoko – and John himself in his 1980 interviews – would describe a relatively serene and domesticated paterfamilias who, to borrow the words that Aunt Mimi forced Hunter Davies to use about her nephew's childhood, 'was happy as the day was long'.[421] The truth surely lay somewhere in between. John had always been at the mercy of his mood swings. Now that he had altered so completely his reason for living, and for the first time since his teens was no longer an active musician, ups and downs were inevitable as he adjusted his head to the new routine. As he was to say, at least he had chosen 'not to take the standard options in my business – going to Vegas and singing your great hits, if you're lucky, or going to hell, which is where Elvis went.'[422]

Over the next three years or so, although a nanny took care of the less pleasant duties, John spent a great deal of his time with Sean, playing with him, getting food into him and giving him cuddles. While the baby was sleeping or with the nanny, John would read voraciously or watch TV, and initially at least, he made occasional excursions to see May Pang. He liked to stand up and sway to music while he gave Sean his bottle, as he had noticed the black nurses do in the hospital. Life now revolved around mealtimes. 'He didn't come out of my belly,' he said about Sean, 'but by God I made his bones!' [423] For some reason John would become famous for baking bread, though it didn't last long: 'I enjoyed it, and I looked on it as . . . an absolute discipline, and that's how I approached it. Through that I got into a whole new world.' [424] John was never really to make it as a good cook, vegetable stews and rice being the height of his culinary achievements.

Back in England, near the end of March 1976, Pauline Lennon informed the Apple office that John's father, now 64, was seriously ill. When John got the message he telephoned at once. Freddie was relieved to hear his unpredictable son sounding warm and friendly. He remembered to congratulate him on the birth of Sean and mentioned that he now had another little lad himself, aged two and a half. John responded, 'You cheeky old bastard!' [425] Father and son chatted away for a few more minutes, mostly about music, and promised each other to meet when Freddie got out of hospital. It was only after speaking to the doctor that John learned that his father was in the last stage of cancer. Afterwards Pauline could see that Freddie had been very touched by the call. He died within days, on 1 April, surrounded by flowers sent by John. A little while later, a parcel arrived at the Dakota containing a manuscript of 150,000 words.

There was a covering letter, dated 1971, which began, 'Dear John, By the time you read this letter I will already be dead . . .' After some sharp remarks about Mimi's censorship of John's early life, it continued: 'Since last we met on the occasion of your thirtieth birthday I have been haunted by the image of you screaming for your Daddy and it is my sincere hope that when you have read this book you will no longer bear me any malice. Perhaps the revelations in my life story may bring you a clearer picture

218

of how fate and circumstance control so much of our lives and therefore must be considered in our judgement of one another. Until we meet again, some time, some place, Your Father, Freddie Lennon.'[426]

John's feelings when he read his father's version of events (the gist of which is discussed elsewhere in this book) can only be imagined. He spoke long distance to Mimi, interrogating her about why she had distorted and suppressed so many important facts about his childhood and parentage. Remarkably, his aunt's response was preserved on cassette, and with Yoko's authorisation would reach the public domain just weeks after Mimi died in 1991, when an American radio network broadcast the tape as part of a series about John. Shocked and deeply upset by John's questions, Mimi had reacted, not by answering them but, true to form, by going on the attack: 'I hated it, what the Beatles did to you,' she said bitterly. 'As soon as you started to make money, your character, your personality, everything, was altered. And it seemed as though you hated the sight of me . . . But you were very kind to Alfred Lennon, taking him around the West End and having him in your home. I don't suppose it ever crossed your mind that that would hurt me, especially when you couldn't stand the sight of me.'[427] And there was a good deal more. John was left with only one possible response, the one that he had always in the end adopted with Mimi. He made peace with her.

Not long after Sean was born, almost all of John's outside connections had begun withering away. Mick Jagger, though he was in the Dakota anyway one day, was not invited in. When Pete Shotton appeared in New York, they of course had to meet, but John told him that he had consulted his numerologist before agreeing to do so. Even Paul received the cold shoulder when he turned up unannounced with his guitar once too often. John wryly gave himself the doubly reclusive nickname of Greta Hughes. But in the personal politics of his domestic life John was no hermit. It was simply that, Yoko aside, everyone else had become much less important to him than Sean. Father and son used to go out

John stepping out with Yoko, in his Quarry Bank tie

together, chatting with people they encountered on walks in Central Park, and often they stopped for coffee and an ice cream at the Café La Fortuna on West 71st Street (where the friendly proprietor tried to interest John in singers of Freddie Lennon's generation, such as Mae West and Al Jolson.) With Sean, John was for the first time experiencing that magical closeness that is perhaps only possible between a child under about five and a parent, laughing, teasing, being serious. Their time together was a valuable exercise of the love that had been rare or absent in three generations of male Lennons. During the last interview of his life John would delightedly tell RKO Radio that, one day, while they were both lying on the bed, Sean had 'sat up and said, "You know what I want to be when I grow up?" And I said, "No, what is that?" He looked me right in the eye and said, "Just a daddy".'[428]

Though Yoko (now 'Mother' to both of them) sometimes would come out for coffee with her boys, she spent most days in an office elsewhere in the Dakota. A formidable negotiator, she had taken over the financial side of the family, in charge of every aspect of John's residual Beatles business, as well as that of his solo career. She was acquiring dizzying numbers of paintings and art objects, Egyptian artefacts and valuable furs, all good investments, and she was buying property. The Lennons would soon own historic houses or mansions on Long Island, in Palm Beach and in the mountains of New York State, as well as five Dakota apartments packed with treasures and even four farms (which every week supplied them with fresh organic produce). Yoko depended on her astrologer, John Green, to tell her when to buy or sell anything, and the method seems to work. In June 1980, for example, the price she was paid for a single (pedigree) cow would make it into the *Guinness Book of Records*. By that time, the Lennons' riches were legendary. Elton had the courage to tease John about it in a 40th birthday card, which bore the message:

> Imagine six apartments
> It isn't hard to do
> One is full of fur coats
> The other's full of shoes.[429]

After 27 July 1976, when John had been granted the right to live permanently in the USA, he could at last come and go whenever he liked. To see whether the Green Card worked, as he put it, he flew on his own to Singapore and Hong Kong, where he did very little apart from send postcards ('Far East, man!')[430] The Green Card did indeed work, and so over the next few years John frequently left the States, most often with Yoko and Sean to Japan where they had long family holidays together, but also alone to South Africa, Germany and Spain. Though it was mooted several times, John did not go to Britain, however. In January 1980 he wrote to a cousin: 'I'm almost scared to go to England, 'cos I know it would be the last time I saw Mimi & I'm a coward about goodbyes.'[431] Mimi, now in her 70s but with over ten years to live, was still living on her own in her bungalow in Dorset, where most days John spoke to her by telephone. But if he could not quite bring himself to return home to see his aunt, he had done the next best thing by inviting her to come and live in New York. When she refused, he persuaded her to pack up and send him as many of the things that he remembered from Mendips as she could spare – pictures, crockery, even the grandfather clock (which had come from Uncle George's side of the family). She had already posted him his old Quarry Bank tie, and he had taken to wearing it on special occasions.

John claimed in 1980 that all this time he had almost never taken his guitar down from its hook behind the bed. Sean later remembered otherwise: 'Dad would play guitar and I would sit on his lap,' he said. 'He was very sharing with music. We'd sing constantly.'[432] During these so-called silent years John in fact taped dozens of songs, new and old, accompanying himself on guitar or piano; the only real difference was that now he no longer brought this raw material to the studio for completion. By June 1978 there were enough new songs for the Lennons to announce that they were planning a musical called *The Ballad of John and Yoko*, based on prose writings that John had been doing since 1976. (As this book goes to press, the musical, or one like it, is at last about to open in New York. The original writings would appear, together with disjointed episodes from an abandoned Milliganish novel, in the 1986 collection, *Skywriting By Word of Mouth*, which also reproduced some of John's cartoons from this time.)

John had another rush of light-hearted creativity after

he found a new collaborator who shared his sense of humour, a broadcaster called Elliot Mintz, and they began swapping what they called 'Mind Movies', painstakingly made comedy tapes and sound collages, featuring a French detective, Maurice Dupont, and a host of other odd characters. Though little of this material was ever released, a very funny short extract from one of these mini radio plays can be heard on a 1998 cd, in which John adopts a Peter Sellers Indian accent to play 'The Great Wok', a Maharishi-like guru, speaking words of eastern wisdom – 'One way of looking at it is simply not to look at it at all' – as he solemnly renounces everything 'but complete luxury and self-indulgence.'[433]

By 1979, new life was definitely stirring in the Dakota. As John would tell Paul on the phone, 'This housewife wants a job.'[434] In May, for no apparent reason, a full page newspaper advertisement signed by John and Yoko appeared in New York, London and Tokyo, explaining in unmistakably Onoesque prose that they had been busy spring cleaning their minds, that their silence was 'a silence of love and not of indifference', and that everyone was 'walking in the sky, which extends to the ground'. During the 'spring cleaning', it said, they 'kept finding things in those old closets in our minds that we hadn't realized were still there, things we wished we hadn't found.'[435] John was currently dealing with such unwanted relics by committing them to tape in a memoir that combined recent resentments – that Jagger, Dylan and McCartney were just 'company men',[436] for example – with more painful echoes from his youth (such as his feelings when he had walked in on his mother while she was orally pleasuring Dykins.) With all the things that Mimi had sent from Mendips surrounding him, John's past life remained close to him in the Dakota, and it wasn't just his childhood: he had recently been building up a vast collection of Beatles bootleg records, though he had not yet brought himself to listen to any of them. As he moved towards his 40th birthday, he should have been struck by the famous last line of Fitzgerald's *The Great Gatsby*: 'So we beat on, boats against the current, borne back ceaselessly into the past.'[437]

During the months coming up to that terrible day in December 1980 when Mark Chapman would meet John Lennon outside the Dakota, and take first his autograph and then his life, many of the things that John did and said would assume in retrospect a more or less spurious significance. His dramatic experience as a deep-sea sailor was the most striking. In April, Yoko suggested that John should 'clean out his head', and he obediently spent ten days without speaking, reading or turning up the volume on the television; the transformation was completed on the tenth day when he shaved off his thick beard. Afterwards he looked ten years younger, and the process seemed to give him a burst of energy. Inspired by his recent reading about sailors like Francis Chichester and Thor Heyerdahl, John bought a yacht, the *Royal Isis*, and at the family's summer house on Long Island he worked hard over the next few weeks learning how to sail it, usually accompanied by his assistant, Fred Seaman. (Seaman had been hired the year before, partly because both of his names reminded John of his father.) Then, in June, with three other rather more experienced sailors, John embarked from Newport, Rhode Island, in a 41-foot sailing boat called the *Megan Jayne*. Yoko's ancient Japanese runes had decreed that they could head south-east, so they did, towards Bermuda.

The voyage would remind John of Jason and the Golden Fleece: later he spoke with pride of how, though little more than a cabinboy, he had managed to keep the vessel on course through a whole night of storm, as the rest of the crew groaned below: 'It was my first time at sea: 3,000 miles, seven days. . . . A storm started one afternoon and lasted three days. The captain was sick and so were his two cousins, the other guys on the boat. . . . So I was there, driving the boat, for six hours, keeping it on course. I was buried under water. I was smashed in the face by waves for six solid hours. . . . It's like being on stage – once you're on, there's no gettin' off. A couple of the waves had me on my knees. I was just hanging on with my hands on the wheel – it's *very* powerful weather –

and I was having the time of my life! I was screaming sea shanties and shoutin' at the Gods! . . . When you go on a yacht and you're in the middle of the ocean, you relive all the ocean journeys there ever were – the Vikings', Columbus's.'[438]

The intrepid mariner arrived in Bermuda, buzzing with excitement and confidence, and Sean flew out with Fred to join him. Setting up a makeshift home studio in a rented house by the sea, John began working on songs, some of them new, others that he had written or part-written over the previous few years. He bought a tape machine to record demos, which he played down the telephone to Yoko in the Dakota. He was going to make an album. During a walk in the island's Botanic Gardens, he spotted in a bed of freesias a label reading 'Double Fantasy'. Now he had his title. Yoko was coaxed out to Bermuda, but was in no mood for play, and after a day spent conducting farm business by telephone she left again, complaining of the heat.

Some weeks later John and Sean returned to New York. John was keen to start recording at once and so the Hit Factory Studio was booked for August and September and a handpicked band of musicians hired, including Hugh McCracken and Earl Slick, both of whom had played before with John. The producer he engaged for the project, a pal from LA, Jack Douglas, would later recall that during these sessions John was full of exciting ideas: he hoped for a world tour in 1981 (it would be officially announced on his 40th birthday), and planned 'new arrangements of songs he never got right', such as 'She Loves You' and 'I Want To Hold Your Hand'.[439]

Once in the studio, John was not sure that he had got quite enough material ready. In fact he had more than enough. By the time that the Hit Factory sessions were over he would have recorded over a dozen new songs of his own, already a potential solo album. Even then he would have left untouched much of the most promising taped material from his 'househusband' years, such as the demos that in 1994 the surviving Beatles would turn into hit singles ('Free As A

225

John and Yoko walking in Central Park

Bird' and 'Real Love'), or 'She Is A Friend of Dorothy's', a deliciously irreverent gay anthem from 1976 – which to date can be heard only on bootlegs – or the atmospheric Noël Cowardly piano blues, 'Mr Hyde's Gone (Don't Be Afraid)', with its scalp-tingling opening verse: 'Don't be afraid, It's just the wind at night, Don't be afraid, This house is very strange, In the morning it'll be gone, Don't be afraid.'[440]

Apparently Yoko had been inspired by John's burst of creativity. She surprised him with large numbers of songs of her own, prepared in New York while he was away: she had even made secret demo tapes with Elephant's Memory. As a result, before recording began, both John and Yoko had enough material to fill an album apiece. After much discussion, however, John agreed to include seven songs

226

written and sung by each of them on 'Double Fantasy'. At first his compositions were going to be on one side of the record and Yoko's on the other, but after yet further discussion it was decided that they would contribute alternate tracks, and give the album the subtitle 'A Heart Play'.

Then the serious work of recording began. On 13 August, following a suggestion of John's that they should think about writing something together, Paul McCartney telephoned the studio. He was put through to Yoko. With such a wealth of material, it was obviously unnecessary for her to disturb her busy husband with the call. Paul didn't ring again. Despite some initial nerves, John soon settled down and clearly enjoyed working with a band again. Sometimes, though, his frustration with Yoko would overwhelm him and the old Liverpool toughie would escape for a second – once, when she bungled a phrase she was singing, he is reported to have roared: 'Remember the bridge on the River Kwai, you fuck!'[441]

'Double Fantasy' came out on 17 November. After such a long wait Lennon fans were disappointed by how few of John's songs it contained. Still, the combined album was an idea that might have worked. Yoko's seven songs were seen as ugly but musically interesting, though her lyrics, which as often as not came across as complaints about the shackles of monogamy, sounded contrived. As a singer, her example had already been an unlikely inspiration to female New Wave vocalists such as Lena Lovitch: the style was to achieve artistic maturity in Björk. Apart from 'Yes, I'm Your Angel', an embarrassing rip-off of the 1928 standard 'Making Whoopie' (Yoko would duly be sued – perhaps she thought it was out of copyright), the impeccable, imaginative arrangements and backing that John and Jack Douglas had put together made a virtue of her inability to sing very well or to write lines that fitted the tunes.

Some reviewers preferred Yoko's songs to John's, and accused him of going soft. Certainly, his tone had changed. At a casual hearing, most of his songs come across as simple, tender love ballads, with melodies that insinuate themselves under your skin. In 'Beautiful Boy', a near-lullaby about Sean that is also a hymn to good fatherhood, John faces accusations of schmaltz head-on. But for all the sweetness of the melody, there is nothing sugary about what the song is saying: we must take care of each other for, in the end, all we have is today: 'Before you cross the street Take my hand. Life is what happens to you While you're busy Making other plans.'[442]

John's six other tracks on the album are more complex. Ever since the night of 'Two Virgins' in 1968, when he underwent almost divine fusion with the one he had always been waiting for, John had remained convinced of the essential unity of 'johnandyoko'. In most interviews he said it: they were always 'meant' to be together – 'After all it is written in the stars' is how 'Woman' puts it.[443] That belief had been a central tenet in his life since then, and it never really wavered, not even during the 'Lost Weekend'. There was simply nothing he could do about it. In 'Double Fantasy', John teases out, with bare, helpless honesty, some of the less welcome consequences of this predestined love. He recognizes it as a controlling factor in his own life. In a singing voice of wistful clarity, John goes to the core of what it is that has linked him so irrevocably with Yoko, and discovers that it is something inside himself alone. While he approaches for the first time an awareness that things may not be quite the same for her, these six songs reassure her that the imbalance does not matter, since his belief in their spiritual love remains as strong as ever: it is in fact the very strength of his love that causes him sometimes to hurt her.

So, under nearly all John's expressions of love for Yoko on the album runs an undercurrent of doubt, resignation and even resentment. There is ample evidence that very often she had better things to do than hang around with John. His final track on the album, the rollicking 'Dear Yoko', graphically sums up the dilemma. The last verse concludes: 'After all is really said and done, The two of us are really one: The goddess really smiled upon our love, dear Yoko.' And then, as the music fades out, John can just be heard shouting: 'When you come over next time don't sell a cow! Spend some time

A portrait shot of John in 1980

with me and Sean, you'll like it. Get IN the water!'[444]

On 5 December, as part of the publicity surrounding the very accurately titled 'Double Fantasy', John gave Jonathan Cott of *Rolling Stone* one of his last, and most revealing, interviews. He was looking all the way back to that day at Woolton Fête when he met Paul for the first time: 'There's a photo in all the Beatles books – a picture of me with a checked shirt on, holding a little acoustic guitar – and I am singing "Be Bop A Lula".' Thoughtfully, John continued: 'Sometimes you wonder – I mean, really wonder. I know we make our own reality and we always have a choice, but how much is preordained? Is there always a fork in the road, and are there two paths equally preordained? There could

Many years from now, a photo still from How I Won the War

be hundreds of paths, where one could go this way or that. There's a choice, and it's very strange sometimes.'[445]

Three days later, when he and Yoko returned from the studio just before 11pm, Mark Chapman was waiting for him outside the Dakota. As John reached the entrance, Chapman dropped into combat position, called out 'Mr Lennon', and fired five shots with a revolver. John's last words were 'I'm shot.'

'John Lennon would not have disapproved of the manner of his death because he could not imagine him enjoying any sort of long-term geriatric state' was how *The*

Times reported William Pobjoy's reaction to the murder on its front page the next day.[446] As usual where John Lennon was concerned, his old headmaster at Quarry Bank could not have been more wrong. John had always been greedy for life. He hoped for a long and productive future, though he was not sure, of course, what it might bring. He told one interviewer that he had a vision of being 60 and writing books for children: 'I've always had that feeling of *giving* what *Wind in the Willows* and *Alice in Wonderland* and *Treasure Island* gave to me at age seven and eight. The books that really opened my whole being.'[447] Another interviewer, as usual tactlessly quoting a song of Paul's, wondered what John thought he would be doing 'when I'm 64'. John replied: 'I hope we're a nice old couple living off the coast of Ireland or something like that – looking at our scrapbook of madness.'[448]

This year, 2005, John Lennon would have been 65. Shortly before his death he had asked his Irish solicitor to see about renewing the lapsed planning permission for his house on Dorinish.[449] Who knows what might happened in those 25 years? Perhaps John really would have been there now, the old sailor finally home from the sea, writing crazy, exciting books about pirates in his island palace on the Celtic edge of Europe, and singing new shanties over the wind and the Atlantic waves.

But no. Back in November 1980, John Lennon had composed the last new song he was ever going to sing. It also happened to be the first one that he ever addressed to himself alone, a song of self-forgiveness. He wrote it on his acoustic guitar and recorded it at home. Very simply, in little more than a single, lilting verse, 'Dear John' said it all:[450]

> Dear John
> Don't be hard on yourself,
> Give yourself a break,
> Life wasn't meant to be run,
> The race is over.
> You've won.

Acknowledgements

For their help, advice and ears, I thank the following:
Stephen Bayley, Pete Brennan, Peter Costello, Martin Hughes, Jerry Lidwill, Nigel Mooney, Tony Mulqueen, Patrick Pentland, John Smurthwaite, Peter Thompson and an unsuspecting James Woodall.
For their books, I thank The Berkeley Library, Trinity College, Dublin; The Catholic Central Library, Dublin; and The County Wexford Library Service.
For themselves, I thank Lois Wyse Jackson, Peter Wyse Jackson, Patrick Wyse Jackson, Michael Wyse Jackson, Margery Stapleton, Eoghan Mitchell, Daniel Mathews, Conor Jackson, Adam Jackson, and my wife Ruth.

Further Reading

The following books are among those consulted in the writing of this book. Those with comments added are particularly worth pursuing, though all may profitably be examined and even enjoyed. Where a later edition is listed, the date of the earliest is given in square brackets. Of the hundreds (or thousands) of Beatles-related websites, three that have been useful appear after the books.

Aldridge, Alan (ed), *The Beatles Illustrated Lyrics* [1969, 1971] (Little, Brown, London: 2003)

Badman, Keith, *The Beatles: Off the Record* (Omnibus Press, London: 2000) – *with the next, a vast, indispensable source of reliable material to do with all aspects of the group and its members.*

Badman, Keith, *The Beatles Years, Volume 2: After The Break-Up, 1970-2001* (Omnibus Press, London: 2001)

Baird, Julia with Geoffrey Giuliano, *John Lennon My Brother* [1988] (Jove Books, New York: 1989)

The Beatles Anthology (Cassell, London: 2000) – *a huge (though perhaps over-designed) authorized account of the Beatles years, told largely in the words of the participants; a companion to Apple's 2003 6-dvd documentary compilation of clips and interviews.*
Brown, Peter and Gaines, Steven, *The Love You Make: An Insider's Story Of The Beatles* [1983] (New American Library, New York: 1984)

Clayson, Alan, *John Lennon* (Sanctuary Publishing, London: 2003) – *a lively account, particularly good on the British musical landscape in the 1960s.*

Clayson, Alan and Sutcliffe, Pauline, *Backbeat: Stuart Sutcliffe: The Lost Beatle* (Pan Books, London: 1994)

Coleman, Ray, *Lennon: The Definitive Biography* [1984] (Pan Books, London: 2000) – *nothing is definitive, but though Coleman's uncritical treatment of both John and Yoko damages the book, it remains the essential source.*

Cott, Jonathan and Doudna, Christine (eds), *The Ballad of John and Yoko* (Michael Joseph, London: 1982) – *just a compilation of articles and interviews from* Rolling Stone, *but it gives a clearer picture than most of where John was coming from.*

Davies, Hunter, *The Beatles* [1968] (Cassell Illustrated, London: 2002) – *the authorized account, now much illuminated by a long introduction explaining what he could NOT say then.*

DiLello, Richard, *The Longest Cocktail Party* [1972] (Playboy Press, Chicago: 1974)

Du Noyer, Paul, *John Lennon: Whatever Gets You Through The Night* (Thunder's Mouth Press, New York: 1999)

Epstein, Brian, *A Cellarful of Noise* [1964] (Four Square Books, London: 1965)

Fawcett, Anthony, *John Lennon: One Day at a Time: Revised Edition* (Grove Press, New York: 1980)

Giuliano, Geoffrey, *Lennon in America, 1971-1980* (Robson Books, London: 2001)

Giuliano, Geoffrey, *The Lost Beatles Interviews* (Penguin USA, New York: 1994)

Giuliano, Geoffrey and Brenda, *The Lost Lennon Interviews* (Adams Media Corporation, Holbrook, MA: 1996)

Goldman, Albert, *The Lives of John Lennon* (Bantam Press, London: 1988) – *wonderful research work, beautifully written, but terminally flawed by Goldman's determination to find scandal in every fact he uncovers.*

Harry, Bill, *The John Lennon Encyclopedia* (Virgin Publishing, London:

2000) – *with its 1000+ pages, this, with Harry's many other reference books on the Beatles, is the first port of call for the facts.*

Henke, James, *Lennon Legend: An Illustrated Life of John Lennon* (Weidenfeld & Nicolson, London: 2003) – *a simple account, magically augmented by facsimile Lennon artefacts and a CD of rare interviews.*

Hertsgaard, Mark, *A Day in the Life: The Music and Artistry of the Beatles* [1995] (Pan Books, London: 1996)

Herzogenrath, Wulf and Hansen, Dorothee, *John Lennon: Drawings, Performances, Films* (Thames and Hudson, London: 1995)

Kozinn, Allan, *The Beatles* (Phaidon Press, London: 1995)

Leigh, Spencer, *The Best of Fellas: The Story of Bob Wooler* (Drivegreen Publications, Liverpool: 2002)

Lennon, Cynthia, *A Twist of Lennon* (Star, London: 1978)

Lennon, John, *The Penguin John Lennon* [1964, 1965] (Penguin Books, Harmondsworth: 1968) – *combining* In His Own Write *and* A Spaniard in the Works.

Lennon, John, *Real Love: The Drawings For Sean* (Little, Brown, London: 1999) – *a rather charming picture book posthumously (and perhaps over-creatively) made by colorizing John's late doodles and some earlier drawings.*

Lennon, John, *Skywriting by Word of Mouth* (Pan Books, London: 1986) – *a useful if sometimes chaotic book full of John's later writings from various sources: sometimes very funny, sometimes not.*

Lennon, Pauline, *Daddy, Come Home: The True Story of John Lennon and his Father* (Angus and Robertson: London 1990) – *a very illuminating account by Freddie Lennon's widow, based on his manuscript autobiography. Frustratingly, it nowhere makes clear which are his opinions and which hers.*

Lewisohn, Mark, *The Complete Beatles Chronicle* [1992] (Chancellor Press, London: 1996) – *this invaluable daily account of the group's concerts, recording sessions and media activities, with Lewisohn's other books, is (nurdish) Beatles' scholarship at its most reliable.*

McCabe, Peter and Schonfield, Robert D, *John Lennon: For the Record* (Bantam Books, New York: 1984)

MacDonald, Ian, *Revolution In The Head: The Beatles' Records And The Sixties* (Fourth Estate, London: 1994) – *the most enjoyable and intelligently readable examination of the many useful accounts of their songs.*

Miles, Barry, *The Beatles: A Diary* (Omnibus Press, London: 2002) – *a useful complement to Lewisohn, as it also chronicles something of the group's social life.*

Miles, Barry, *In the Sixties* (Jonathan Cape: London: 2002)

Norman, Philip, *Shout! The True Story of the Beatles* (Hamish Hamilton, London: 1981) – *the best-written of all accounts, though a little pleased with itself (and possibly cavalier with some facts).*

Peebles, Andy, *The Lennon Tapes: John Lennon and Yoko Ono in Conversation with Andy Peebles, 6 December 1980* (BBC Publications, London: 1981)

Pritchard, David and Lysaght, Alan, *The Beatles: An Oral History* (Hyperion, New York: 1998)

Riley, Tim, *Tell Me Why: A Beatles Commentary* [1988] (Da Capo Press, Cambridge, MA: 2002)

Robertson, John, *The Art and Music of John Lennon* (Omnibus Press, London: 1990) – *a fairly dry, but consistently revealing, troll through all John's creative work, including glimpses of the more obscure late home recordings.*

Seaman, Frederic, *John Lennon: Living on Borrowed Time* (Xanadu, London: 1991)

Sheff, David, *Last Interview: All We Are Saying – John Lennon & Yoko Ono* [1981] (Pan Books, London: 2001) – *the 1980* Playboy *interview, and the most reliably revealing of all.*

Shotton, Pete and Schaffner, Nicholas, *The Beatles, Lennon and Me* [1983] (Stein & Day, New York: 1984) – *Pete has fun with his memories of John; an essential source, though some of his stories are so good that it is hard to believe them.*

Solt, Andrew and Egan, Sam, *Imagine: John Lennon* (Bloomsbury, London: 1988) – *a useful compilation of revealing quotations and photographs.*

Taylor, Alistair, *With the Beatles* (John Blake, London: 2003)

Taylor, Derek, *As Time Goes By* [1973] (Abacus, London: 1974)

Taylor, Derek, *It Was Twenty Years Ago Today* (Bantam Press, London: 1987)

Thomson, Elizabeth and Gutman, David (eds), *The Lennon Companion* (Macmillan Press, London: 1987) – *a helpful collection of otherwise elusive critical and documentary material.*

Wenner, Jann, *Lennon Remembers: The* Rolling Stone *Interviews* [1970] (Penguin Books, Harmondsworth: 1973) – *John's angriest interview is endlessly quotable, though he later moderated some of his opinions.*

Wiener, Jon, *Come Together: John Lennon in his Time* (Random House, New York: 1984) – *the only helpful book-length examination of Lennon as a political activist, and a useful source for obscure late material.*

Wiener, Jon. *Gimmie Some Truth: The John Lennon FBI Files* (University of California Press, Berkeley: 1999)

Williams, Allan and Marshall, William, *The Man Who Gave the Beatles Away* [1975] (Ballantine Books, New York: 1977)

http://www.beatles-discography.com – *a treasure trove of reliable statistics, dates, and facts about all aspects of the group from its formation to 1970.*

http://www.iol.ie/~beatlesireland
– *a smallish site that has gathered some unusual and useful material which is not confined to Irish Beatle matters.*

http://www.beatlelinks.net/links/ – *to help you find the others.*

Picture Sources

The author and publishers wish to express their thanks to the following sources of illustrative material and/or permission to reproduce it. They will make proper acknowledgements in future editions in the event that any omissions have occurred.

Akg Images: pp.37, 79, 84, 152, 195, 220; Corbis: p. 15, 180 (Penny Tweedie), 230; Getty Images: pp. 76, 103, 105, 108, 114, 119, 127, 128, 145 (Susan Wood), 157, 162, 168, 173, 177, 187, 213; Lebrecht Picture Library: p. 18; Redferns Music Library: pp. 42, 54, 60, 63, 82, 178, 207, 209; Topham Picturepoint: pp. 22, 28, 66, 91, 96, 98, 124, 138, 143, 190, 211, 226, 229.

Footnotes

References to songs begin with the year the track was recorded.
For web references the URL is followed by the last date on which the item was seen.

[1] Fawcett, *John Lennon*, p 71.

[2] 1963, 'There's A Place', on The Beatles, *Please Please Me*, track 13.

[3] 1967, 'I Am The Walrus', on The Beatles, *The Beatles, 1967-1970*, disc 1, track 8.

[4] *The Beatles Anthology* (Cassell, London: 2000) p 10.

[5] Jon Wiener, *Come Together: John Lennon in his Time* (Random House, New York: 1984) p 209.

[6] *The Beatles Anthology*, p 10.

[7] Quoted in 'Music Hall' at http://207.16.120/theroyal/thebook/drama. html (20 July 2005)

[8] Pauline Lennon, *Daddy, Come Home: The True Story of John Lennon and his Father* (Angus and Robertson, London: 1990) p 13.

[9] *The Mike Douglas Show*, 14-18 February 1972, on cd, *Lennon In His Own Words*, track 1, included with James Henke, *Lennon Legend: An Illustrated Life of John Lennon* (Weidenfeld & Nicolson, London: 2003).

[10] Hunter Davies, *The Beatles* (Cassell Illustrated, London: 2002) p 56.

[11] Lennon, *Daddy, Come Home*, p 31.

[21] Julia Baird with Geoffrey Giuliano, *John Lennon My Brother* (Jove Books, New York: 1989) p 8.

[13] Mimi Smith, 'Remembering John, 1983' in Geoffrey Giuliano, *The Lost Beatles Interviews* (Penguin USA, New York: 1994).

[14] Frederic Seaman, *John Lennon: Living on Borrowed Time* (Xanadu, London: 1991) p 180.

[15] Geoffrey and Brenda Giuliano, *The Lost Lennon Interviews* (Adams Media Corporation, Holbrook, MA: 1996) p 25.

[16] David Sheff, *Last Interview: All We Are Saying – John Lennon & Yoko Ono* (Pan Books, London: 2001) p 161.

[17] John Lennon, quoted in Keith Badman, *The Beatles: Off the Record* (Omnibus Press, London: 2000) p 264.

[18] Andrew Solt and Sam Egan, *Imagine: John Lennon* (Bloomsbury, London: 1988) p 17.

[19] Baird, *John Lennon My Brother*, p 28.

[20] Andy Peebles, *The Lennon Tapes: John Lennon and Yoko Ono in Conversation with Andy Peebles, 6 December 1980* (BBC Publications, London: 1981) p 39.

[21] Solt and Egan, *Imagine* p 17.

[22] Davies, *The Beatles*, p 57.

[23] Lennon, *Daddy, Come Home*, p 73.

[24] Baird, *John Lennon My Brother*, p 22.

[25] Ray Coleman, *Lennon: The Definitive Biography* (Pan Books, London: 2000) p 117.

[26] Bill Harry, *The John Lennon Encyclopedia* (Virgin Publishing, London: 2000) p 207.

[27] John Lennon, *Skywriting by Word of Mouth* (Pan Books, London: 1986) p 96.

[28] Pete Shotton and Nicholas Schaffner, *The Beatles, Lennon and Me* (Stein & Day, New York: 1984) p 30.

[29] Shotton and Schaffner, *The Beatles, Lennon and Me*, p 24.

[30] Sheff, *Last Interview*, p 156.

[31] *The Beatles Anthology*, p 9.

[32] Facsimile issue of *The Daily Howl*, in Henke, *Lennon Legend*, p 8.

[33] Davies, *The Beatles*, p 98.

[34] Facsimile report card (Christmas 1955) in Henke, *Lennon Legend*, p 8.

[35] Albert Goldman, *The Lives of John Lennon* (Bantam Press, London: 1988) p 56.

[36] *The Beatles Anthology*, p 10.

[37] Goldman, *The Lives of John Lennon*, p 37.

[38] Shotton and Schaffner, *The Beatles, Lennon and Me*, p 58.

[39] 1967, 'She's Leaving Home', on The Beatles, *Sgt Pepper's Lonely Hearts Club Band*, track 6.

[40] *The Beatles Anthology*, p 11.

[41] Badman, *The Beatles: Off the Record*, p 12.

[42] Remembered by Paul McCartney in *The Beatles Anthology*, p 96.

[43] *The Beatles Anthology*, p 11.

[44] Shotton and Schaffner, *The Beatles, Lennon and Me*, p 340.

[45] *The Beatles Anthology*, p 12.

[46] Shotton and Schaffner, *The Beatles, Lennon and Me*, p 61.

[47] Philip Norman, *Shout! The True Story of the Beatles* (Hamish Hamilton, London: 1981) p 36.

[48] Davies, *The Beatles*, p 64.

[49] *The Beatles Anthology*, p 10.

[50] Jonathan Cott, 'The Last Rolling Stone Interview', *Rolling Stone*, 5 December 1980.

[51] Norman, *Shout!*, p 31.

[52] Davies, *The Beatles*, p 45.

[53] Sheff, *Last Interview*, p 159.

[54] *The Beatles Anthology*, p 30.

[55] *The Beatles Anthology*, p 13.

[56] Baird, *John Lennon My Brother*, p 55.

[57] Davies, *The Beatles*, p 99.

[58] 1963, 'It Won't Be Long', on The Beatles, *With the Beatles*, track 1.

[59] *The Beatles Anthology*, p 13.

[60] Miles, *John Lennon in his Own Words* (Omnibus Press, London: 1980) p 19.

[61] Alan Clayson and Pauline Sutcliffe, *Backbeat: Stuart Sutcliffe: The Lost*

Beatle (Pan Books, London: 1994) p 47.

[62] Harry, *The John Lennon Encyclopedia*, p 56.

[63] Sheff, *Last Interview*, p 25.

[64] Davies, *The Beatles*, p 97.

[65] John Lennon, letter sent to Stephen Bayley, late August 1967.

[66] David Ashton, 'The Vanished World of a Woolton Childhood with John Lennon' at www.iol.ie/~beatlesireland/Lennon/lennonindex.htm (25 February 2005).

[67] Davies, *The Beatles*, p 98.

[68] Andy Peebles, *The Lennon Tapes*, p 56.

[69] Davies, *The Beatles*, p 99.

[70] 1967, 'Getting Better', on The Beatles, *Sgt Pepper's Lonely Hearts Club Band*, track 4.

[71] *The Beatles Anthology*, p 23.

[72] Goldman, *The Lives of John Lennon*, p 84.

[73] Clayson and Sutcliffe, *Backbeat*, p 52.

[74] Sheff, *Last Interview*, p 158.

[75] *Sunday People*, 24 July 1960.

[76] 1960, 'You'll Be Mine', on The Beatles, *Anthology 1*, disc 1, track 7.

[77] Alan Clayson and Spencer Leigh, *The Walrus Was Ringo: 101 Beatles Myths Debunked* (Chrome Dreams, New Maldon: 2003) p 26.

[78] Henke, *Lennon Legend*, p 12.

[79] 1967, 'It's Getting Better', on The Beatles, *Sgt Pepper's Lonely Hearts Club Band*, track 4.

[80] '20 May 1960' at www.beatles-discography.com/1960.html (15 February 2005).

[81] From the *Birkenhead News*, Heswall and Neston edition, 11 June 1960, quoted in Mark Lewisohn, *The Complete Beatles Chronicle* (Chancellor Press, London: 1992) p 19.

[82] Alan Clayson, *John Lennon* (Sanctuary Publishing, London: 2003) p 30.

[83] Quoted on *Soul Deep*, a music documentary shown on BBC2, 7 May 2005.

[84] Jann Wenner, *Lennon Remembers: The Rolling Stone Interviews* (Penguin Books, Harmondsworth: 1973) p 14.

[85] John Lennon, quoted in Badman, *The Beatles: Off the Record*, p 25.

[86] Peter McCabe and Robert D Schonfield, *John Lennon: For the Record* (Bantam Books, New York: 1984) p 84.

[87] *The Beatles Anthology*, p 49.

[88] George Harrison, quoted in Barry Miles, *The Beatles: a Diary* (Omnibus Press, London: 2002) p 25.

[89] McCabe and Schonfield, *John Lennon: For the Record*, p 86.

[90] Wenner, *Lennon Remembers*, p 82.

[91] Coleman, *Lennon*, p 221.

[92] Clayson, *John Lennon*, p 68.

[93] Davies, *The Beatles*, p 139.

[94] Spencer Leigh, *The Best of Fellas: The Story of Bob Wooler* (Drivegreen Publications, Liverpool: 2002) p 108.

[95] '27 December 1960' at www.beatles-discography.com/1960.html (15 February 2005).

[96] John Lennon, quoted in *The Beatles Anthology*, p 56.

[97] Bob Wooler, quoted in Leigh, *The Best of Fellas,* p 146.

[98] 1968, 'What About Brian Epstein?', song fragment (aka 'Brian Epstein Blues') improvised by John Lennon on 19 July 1968, only issued on bootlegs.

[99] Leigh, *The Best of Fellas,* p 108.

[100] Davies, *The Beatles*, p 111.

[101] '7 August 1957' at www.beatles-discography.com/1957.html (15 February 2005).

[102] Shotton and Schaffner, *The Beatles, Lennon and Me*, p 128.

[103] 'An Interview with Stanley Parkes' at www.lennon.net/reflections/s_parkes.shtml (10 February 2005).

[104] Coleman, *Lennon*, p 246.

[105] '9 February 1961' at www.beatles-discography.com/1961.html (15 February 2005).

[106] Lewisohn, *The Complete Beatles Chronicle*, p 32.

[107] Coleman, *Lennon*, p 215.

[108] Harry, *The John Lennon Encyclopedia*, p 624-5.

[109] Harry, *The John Lennon Encyclopedia*, p 628.

[110] Harry, *The John Lennon Encyclopedia*, p 623.

[111] Miles, *The Beatles: a Diary*, p 39.

[112] Brian Epstein, *A Cellarful of Noise* (Four Square Books, London: 1965) p 46-7.

[113] Wenner, *Lennon Remembers*, p 45, and 1970, The Beatles, 'Anthology 1', track 29.

[114] Epstein, *A Cellarful of Noise*, p 93.

[115] Epstein, *A Cellarful of Noise*, p 33.

[116] Shotton and Schaffner, *The Beatles, Lennon and Me*, p 138.

[117] Harry, *The John Lennon Encyclopedia*, p 231.

[118] Coleman, *Lennon*, p 320.

[119] Coleman, *Lennon*, p 265.

[120] Lewisohn, *The Complete Beatles Chronicle*, p 61.

[121] Harry, *The John Lennon Encyclopedia*, p 230.

[122] Coleman, *Lennon*, p 266.

[123] Lewisohn, *The Complete Beatles Chronicle*, p 54.

[124] *The Beatles Anthology*, p 73.

[125] Badman, *The Beatles: Off the Record*, p 38.

[126] Lewisohn, *The Complete Beatles Chronicle*, p 55.

[127] '9 May 1962' at www.beatles-discography.com/1962.html (15 February 2005). [128] Coleman, *Lennon*, p 296.

[129] Davies, *The Beatles*, p 156.

[130] Coleman, *Lennon*, p 268.

[131] 'The Tomorrow Show' with Tom Snyder, April 1975, quoted in Solt and Egan, *Imagine* p 63.

[132] Leigh, *The Best of Fellas*, p 161.

[133] Sheff, *Last Interview*, p 167.

[134] *The Beatles Anthology*, p 70.

[135] Quoted in UK TV documentary, 'The Beatles' Biggest Secrets', Channel 5, 29 December 2004.

[136] Cynthia Lennon, *A Twist of Lennon* (Star, London: 1978) p 73.

[137] *The Beatles Anthology*, p 73.

[138] Coleman, *Lennon*, p 282.

[139] Davies, *The Beatles*, p 201.

[140] '23 August 1962' at www.beatles-discography.com/1962.html (15 February 2005).

[141] Badman, *The Beatles: Off the Record*, p 42.

[142] '5 October 1962' at www.beatles-discography.com/1962.html (15 February 2005).

[143] Clayson, *John Lennon*, p 96.

[144] '12 October 1962' at www.beatles-discography.com/1962.html (15 February 2005).

[145] Sheff, *Last Interview*, p 168.

[146] Badman, *The Beatles: Off the Record*, p 51.

[147] John Lennon, quoted in Davies, *The Beatles*, p 218.

[148] Miles, *The Beatles: a Diary*, p 61.

[149] '28 April 1963', at www.beatles-discography.com/1963.html (15 February 2005).

[150] Miles, *The Beatles: a Diary*, p 73.

[151] Leigh, *The Best of Fellas,* p 183.

[152] Miles, *The Beatles: a Diary*, p 73.

[153] 'Henry and Harry' in John Lennon, *The Penguin John Lennon* (Penguin Books, Harmondsworth: 1968) p 62.

[154] 1964, 'A Hard Day's Night', on The Beatles, *A Hard Day's Night*, track 1.

[155] Wenner, *Lennon Remembers*, p 99.

[156] 'George Harrison – In His Own Words' at www.superseventies.com/ssgeorgeharrison.html (30 July 2005)

[157] Davies, *The Beatles*, p 231.

[158] 'The Beatles Anthology' (6-disc DVD, Apple, 2003), disc 1, part 2.

[159] 'The Beatles Anthology' (6-disc DVD, Apple, 2003), disc 1, part 2.

[160] *The Beatles Anthology*, p 145.

[161] *The Beatles Anthology*, p 105.

[162] Miles, *The Beatles: a Diary*, p 86.

[163] Epstein, *A Cellarful of Noise*, p 93.

[164] Miles, *The Beatles: a Diary*, p 94.

[165] Ronald Hayman, 'Donal McCann', *The Times*, 23 October 1971, p 9.

[166] *Record Mirror*, 7 November 1963.

[167] '9 November 1963' at www.beatles-discography.com/1963.html (15 February 2005).

[168] Badman, *The Beatles: Off the Record*, p 119.

[169] Listed in Lewisohn, *The Complete Beatles Chronicle*, pp 361-365.

[170] Unsigned (William Mann), 'What songs The Beatles sang . . .' in Elizabeth Thomson and David Gutman (eds), *The Lennon Companion* (Macmillan Press, London: 1987) pp 27-29, reprinted from *The Times*, 27 December 1963, p 4.

[171] *Sunday Times*, 29 December 1963.

[172] Peter Brown and Steven Gaines, *The Love You Make: An Insider's Story Of The Beatles* (New American Library, New York: 1984) p 108.

[173] John Lennon, quoted in Davies, *The Beatles*, p 232.

[174] John Lennon, quoted in Badman, *The Beatles: Off the Record*, p 87.

[175] Badman, *The Beatles: Off the Record*, p 86.

[176] *The Beatles Anthology*, p 133.

[177] Tom Wolfe, 'A highbrow under all that hair?' in Thomson and Gutman (eds), *The Lennon Companion*, p 47, reprinted from *Book Week*, 3 May 1964, pp 4, 10.

[178] Jean Shepherd, 'Playboy Interview: The Beatles', in *Playboy*, February 1965.

[179] Sheff, *Last Interview*, p 163.

[180] Shotton and Schaffner, *The Beatles, Lennon and Me*, p 184.

[181] Lennon, 'Our Dad' in *The Penguin John Lennon*, p 147.

[182] *The Beatles Anthology*, p 139.

[183] *The Beatles Anthology*, p 143.

[184] *The Beatles Anthology*, p 128.

[185] Quoted in Miles, *The Beatles: a Diary*, p 134.

[186] Ian MacDonald, *Revolution In The Head: The Beatles' Records And The Sixties* (Fourth Estate, London: 1994), p 90.

[187] 1964, I'll Cry Instead', on The Beatles, *A Hard Day's Night*, track 9.

[188] '14 January 1964' at www.beatles-discography.com/1964.html (15 February 2005).

[189] *The Beatles Anthology*, p 160.

[190] Al Aronowitz, quoted in Badman, *The Beatles: Off the Record*, p 120.

[191] Badman, *The Beatles: Off the Record*, p 120.

[192] '28 August 1964' at www.beatles-discography.com/1964.html (15 February 2005).

[193] '4 December 1964' at www.beatles-discography.com/1964.html (15 February 2005).

[194] Clayson and Leigh, *The Walrus Was Ringo*, p 209.

[195] *The Beatles Anthology*, p 167.

[196] Alan Aldridge (ed), *The Beatles Illustrated Lyrics* (Little, Brown, London: 2003) p 80.

[197] *The Beatles Anthology*, p 158.

[198] *The Beatles Anthology*, p 176.

[199] Badman, *The Beatles: Off the Record*, p 147.

[200] Badman, *The Beatles: Off the Record*, p 147.

[201] Miles, *The Beatles: a Diary*, p 167.

[202] 1965, 'Help!', on The Beatles, *Help!*, track 1.

[203] Coleman, *Lennon*, p 345.

[204] The following very early scientific description of the effects of lysergic acid diethylamide (LSD) would almost exactly chart John Lennon's progress 1966-1969:

Sensory changes, including alterations in intensity in attention, imagery, and hallucinations; transient feelings of anxiety, excitement, despair, power, terror, release, clam, intoxication, euphoria or detachment, new perspectives about oneself, including insights, recollections, redefinitions, acceptances or rejection; new views or emotions about others; . . . reduction of tension, anxiety or anger, reduced competitiveness or increased depression; shifts of interest, including reduced work interests and goal striving, increased artistic or philosophical concerns, greater preoccupation with internal events and self, and greater interest in drugs per se; and new integrative experiences, which may be culturally acceptable, psychotically delusional or mystically religious.

R Blum (ed), *Utopiates* (Tavistock, London: 1965) pp 265-6.

[205] Miles, *The Beatles: a Diary*, p 167.

[206] *The Beatles Anthology*, p 169.

[207] '15 August 1965' at www.beatles-discography.com/1965.html (15 February 2005).

[208] Coleman, *Lennon*, p 372.

[209] '27 August 1965' at www.beatles-discography.com/1965.html (15 February 2005).

[210] *The Beatles Anthology*, p 183.

[211] McCabe and Schonfield, *John Lennon: For the Record*, p 109.

[212] 1965, 'Girl', on The Beatles, *Rubber Soul*, track 9.

[213] 1965, 'The Word', on The Beatles, *Rubber Soul*, track 6.

[214] MacDonald, *Revolution In The Head*, p 152.

[215] 1966, 'Tomorrow Never Knows', on The Beatles, *Revolver*, track 14.

[216] 1966, 'Rain', on The Beatles, *Rarities*, track 10.

[217] 1964, 'That's My Life (My Love and Home)', Freddie Lennon, 'A' side.

[218] Maureen Cleave, 'How does a Beatle live? John Lennon lives like this', in Thomson and Gutman (eds), *The Lennon Companion*, pp 71-75, reprinted from the *Evening Standard*, London, 4 March 1966, p 10.

[219] David Pritchard and Alan Lysaght, *The Beatles: An Oral History* (Hyperion, New York: 1998) p 220.

[220] Lennon, *Skywriting by Word of Mouth*, p 18.

[221] John Lennon, quoted in Derek Taylor, *As Time Goes By* (Abacus, London: 1974) p 109.

[222] Badman, *The Beatles: Off the Record*, p 247.

[223] 1966, 'Strawberry Fields Forever', on *The Beatles, 1967-1970*, disc 1, track 1.

[224] 1966, 'Strawberry Fields Forever (Take 1)', on The Beatles, *Anthology 2*, disc 2, track 1.

[225] *The Beatles Anthology*, p 231.

[226] Badman, *The Beatles: Off the Record*, p 256.

[227] *The Beatles Anthology*, p 197.

[228] *The Beatles Anthology*, p 241.

[229] *The Beatles Anthology*, p 241.

[230] John Robertson, *The Art and Music of John Lennon* (Omnibus Press, London: 1990) p 67.

[231] 1967, 'It's Getting Better', on The Beatles, *Sgt Pepper's Lonely Hearts Club Band*, track 4.

[232] 1967, 'A Day In The Life', on The Beatles, *Sgt Pepper's Lonely Hearts Club Band*, track 13.

[233] Badman, *The Beatles: Off the Record*, p 288.

[234] Badman, *The Beatles: Off the Record*, p 276.

[235] Barry Miles, *Paul McCartney: Many Years from Now* (Holt, New York: 1997).

[236] *The Beatles Anthology*, p 257.

[237] Badman, *The Beatles: Off the Record*, p 478.

[238] Shotton and Schaffner, *The Beatles, Lennon and Me*, p 253.

[239] Brown and Gaines, *The Love You Make*, p 243.

[240] Derek Taylor, *It Was Twenty Years Ago Today* (Bantam Press, London: 1987) p 132.

[241] Brown and Gaines, *The Love You Make*, p 219.

[242] Interview with Brian Epstein, *Melody Maker*, 5 August 1967.

[243] *The Beatles Anthology*, p 268

[244] Badman, *The Beatles: Off the Record*, p 304.

[245] Badman, *The Beatles: Off the Record*, p 304.

[246] Lennon, *Daddy, Come Home*, p 135.

[247] *The Beatles Anthology*, p 272

[248] Shotton and Schaffner, *The Beatles, Lennon and Me*, p 218.

[249] 1967, 'I Am The Walrus', on *The Beatles, 1967-1970*, disc 1, track 8.

[250] John Lennon, letter sent to Stephen Bayley, late August 1967.

[251] Badman, *The Beatles: Off the Record*, p 319.

[252] *The Beatles Anthology*, p 268.

[253] *The Beatles Anthology*, p 258.

[254] Badman, *The Beatles: Off the Record*, p 353.

[255] Wenner, *Lennon Remembers*, p 84.

[256] Lennon, *Skywriting by Word of Mouth*, p 101.

[257] '19 February 1968' at www.beatles-discography.com/1968.html (15 February 2005).

[258] *The Beatles Anthology*, p 284.

[259] Ben Fong-Torres, 'A Chronology', in Jonathan Cott and Christine

Doudna (eds), *The Ballad of John and Yoko* (Michael Joseph, London: 1982) p 33.

[260] Coleman, *Lennon*, p 456.
[261] Yoko Ono, *Grapefruit: A Book of Instructions* (Winternaum Press, Tokyo: 1964), unpaginated.
[262] Badman, *The Beatles: Off the Record*, p 347.
[263] *The Beatles Anthology*, p 286.
[264] Shotton and Schaffner, *The Beatles, Lennon and Me*, p 323.
[265] 1967, 'Julia', on The Beatles, *The Beatles (The White Album)*, disc 1, track 17.
[266] Taylor, *It Was Twenty Years Ago Today*, p 177.
[267] Alan Sillitoe, 'Introduction', in Robert Tressell, *The Ragged Trousered Philanthropists* (Panther Books, London: 1965), p 7.
[268] Lewisohn, *The Complete Beatles Chronicle*, p 277.
[269] Anthony Fawcett, *John Lennon: One Day at a Time* (Grove Press, New York: 1980) p 33.
[270] *The Beatles Anthology*, p 299.
[271] Badman, *The Beatles: Off the Record*, p 368.
[272] Quoted in Robert E Dallos, 'Beatles strike serious note in press talk', in Thomson and Gutman (eds), *The Lennon Companion*, p 78, reprinted from the *New York Times*, 23 August 1966, p 30.
[273] Wiener, *Come Together*, p 53.
[274] *The Beatles Anthology*, p 299.
[275] 1967, 'Revolution', on *The Beatles, 1967-1970*, disc 1, track 14.
[276] Quoted in Tim Riley, *Tell Me Why: A Beatles Commentary* (Da Capo Press, Cambridge, MA: 2002) p 257.
[277] 1967,'Revolution 1', on *'The White Album'*), disc 2, track 1.
[278] Wiener, *Come Together*, p 61.
[279] Fawcett, *John Lennon*, p 25.
[280] Wulf Herzogenrath and Dorothee Hansen, *John Lennon: Drawings, Performances, Films* (Thames and Hudson, London: 1995) p 160.
[281] John Lennon, letter to Canon Stephen Verney, 28 June 1968, in Herzogenrath and Hansen, *John Lennon*, p 159.
[282] 'John Lennon and Dorinish Island' at http://www.iol.ie/~beatlesireland/irish/irish1/dorinishisland.htm (30 July 2005).
[283] 'Mayo News' reporter, 'Beatle was "enchanted" with Mulranny visit', *Mayo News*, 29 June 1968, quoted in James M Moran, *Still a Dream, Miscellany on Hippie Commune of Dorinish Island . . .* (Moran/Cartur Publications, Roscommon: 1995). 1995) pp 6-7
[284] Fong-Torres, 'A Chronology', in Cott and Doudna (eds), *The Ballad of John and Yoko*, p 34.
[285] Herzogenrath and Hansen, *John Lennon*, p 164.
[286] Fawcett, *John Lennon*, p 36.
[287] Robertson, *The Art and Music of John Lennon*, p 95.
[288] Quoted in Harry, *The John Lennon Encyclopedia*, pp 915-916.

[289] Charles McCarry, 'John Rennon's Excrusive Gloupie', *Esquire*, December 1970, p 248.
[290] Lennon, *Skywriting by Word of Mouth*, p 39. The piece first appeared on the Beatles' 1968 Christmas Record, issued only to Fan Club members on flexidisc.
[291] 'Today' show, 29 August 1975, quoted in Wiener, *Come Together*, p 80.
[292] *The Beatles Anthology*, p 304.
[293] *The Beatles Anthology*, p 302.
[294] Harry, *The John Lennon Encyclopedia*, p 940.
[295] Miles, *John Lennon in his Own Words*, p 74.
[296] *The Beatles Anthology*, p 301.
[297] Pritchard and Lysaght, *The Beatles: An Oral History*, p 266-267.
[298] MacDonald, *Revolution In The Head*, p 230.
[299] Coleman, *Lennon*, p 521.
[300] Quoted by Francie Schwartz in Giuliano, *The Lost Lennon Interviews*, p 223.
[301] Herzogenrath and Hansen, *John Lennon*, p 176.
[302] Miles, *John Lennon in his Own Words*, p 83.
[303] 1969, 'Come Together', on The Beatles, *Abbey Road*, track 1
[304] Lewisohn, *The Complete Beatles Chronicle*, p 310.
[305] *The Beatles Anthology*, p 317.
[306] Michael Lindsay-Hogg, quoted in Doug Sulphy and Ray Schweighardt, *Get Back: The Beatles' Let It Be Disaster* (Helter Skelter Publishing, London: 1998) p 131.
[307] Fawcett, *John Lennon*, p 51.
[308] 1969, 'The Ballad Of John And Yoko', on *The Beatles, 1967-1970*, disc 2, track 6.
[309] Neville Stannard and John Tobler, *Working Class Heroes: The History of the Beatles' Solo Recordings* (Virgin Books, London: 1983) p 15.
[310] Fong-Torres, 'A Chronology', in Cott and Doudna (eds), *The Ballad of John and Yoko*, p 36.
[311] Harry, *The John Lennon Encyclopedia*, p 940.
[312] 1969, 'Give Peace A Chance', on John Lennon, *Lennon Legend: The Very Best Of John Lennon*, track 20.
[313] Wenner, *Lennon Remembers*, p 110.
[314] Quoted in Wiener, *Come Together*, p 97.
[315] Goldman, *The Lives of John Lennon*, p 518.
[316] 1969, 'Come Together', on The Beatles, *Abbey Road*, track 1.
[317] 1969, 'Come Together', on The Beatles, *Anthology 3*, disc 2, track 17.
[318] 1969, 'The End', on *Abbey Road*, track 16.
[319] Harry, *The John Lennon Encyclopedia*, p 897.
[320] Fawcett, *John Lennon*, p 100.
[321] Lennon, *Skywriting by Word of Mouth*, p 43.
[322] Alan Travis, 'Lennon's art showed a sick mind, said Yard', *The Guardian*, 26 January 2001.
[323] Wenner, *Lennon Remembers*, p 179.

[224] Henke, *Lennon Legend*, p 45.

[325] Robertson, *The Art and Music of John Lennon*, p 113.

[326] Lewisohn, *The Complete Beatles Chronicle*, p 337.

[327] Fong-Torres, 'A Chronology', in Cott and Doudna (eds), *The Ballad of John and Yoko*, p 37.

[328] 1969, 'Cold Turkey', on *Lennon Legend: The Very Best Of John Lennon*, track 6.

[329] Fawcett, *John Lennon*, p 57.

[330] Coleman, *Lennon*, p 524.

[331] Fawcett, *John Lennon*, p 57.

[332] Paul Du Noyer, *John Lennon: Whatever Gets You Through The Night* (Thunder's Mouth Press, New York: 1999) p 58.

[333] Quoted in Wiener, *Come Together*, p 113.

[334] Ritchie Yorke, 'John, Yoko and Year One' in Cott and Doudna (eds), *The Ballad of John and Yoko*, p 62.

[335] Riley, *Tell Me Why*, p 371.

[336] 1970, 'Instant Karma', on *Lennon Legend: The Very Best Of John Lennon*, track 2.

[337] Coleman, *Lennon*, p 551.

[338] Badman, *The Beatles: Off the Record*, p 487.

[339] Davies, *The Beatles*, p 332.

[340] Sheff, *Last Interview*, p 125.

[341] Wenner, *Lennon Remembers*, p 20.

[342] Bill Harry, *The Paul McCartney Encyclopedia* (Virgin Books, London: 2002) p 559.

[343] Yorke, 'John, Yoko and Year One' in Cott and Doudna (eds), *The Ballad of John and Yoko*, p 64.

[344] *Disc and Music Echo*, 9 November 1969, quoted in Clayson, *John Lennon*, p 193.

[345] *The Beatles Anthology*, p 348.

[346] See MacDonald, *Revolution In The Head*, p 272.

[347] 1969, 'Dig it', on The Beatles, *Let It Be*, track 5.

[348] Wenner, *Lennon Remembers*, p 120.

[349] Clayson, *John Lennon*, p 165.

[350] *The Beatles Anthology*, p 332.

[351] Arthur Janov in interview with John Harris in *Mojo* (2000; John Lennon special), quoted at http://homepage.ntlworld.com/carousel/pob11.html (15 February 2005).

[352] 1980, 'Woman', on John Lennon and Yoko Ono, *Double Fantasy*, track 10.

[353] Harry, *The John Lennon Encyclopedia*, p 434

[354] Wenner, *Lennon Remembers*, p 24.

[355] Harry, *The John Lennon Encyclopedia*, p 434.

[356] Lennon, *Daddy, Come Home*, pp 177-181.

[357] Mark Hertsgaard, *A Day in the Life: The Music and Artistry of the Beatles* (Pan Books, London: 1996) p 307.

[358] 1970, 'Remember', on John Lennon, *John Lennon Anthology*, disc 1 (Ascot), track 8.

[359] 1970, 'Remember', on John Lennon and the Plastic Ono Band, *John Lennon/Plastic Ono Band*, track 6.

[360] 1970, 'Mother', on *John Lennon/Plastic Ono Band*, track 1.

[361] 1970, 'I Found Out', on *John Lennon/Plastic Ono Band*, track 3.

[362] *The Beatles Anthology*, p 10.

[363] 1970, 'Working Class Hero', on *John Lennon/Plastic Ono Band*, track 4.

[364] 1970, 'God', on *John Lennon/Plastic Ono Band*, track 10.

[365] Wenner, *Lennon Remembers*, p 140.

[366] Pete Hamill, 'Long Night's Journey into Day', in Cott and Doudna (eds), *The Ballad of John and Yoko*, pp 145-146.

[367] Robertson, *The Art and Music of John Lennon*, p 136.

[368] 1971, 'Give Me Some Truth', on John Lennon and The Plastic Ono Band (with The Flux Fiddlers), *Imagine*, track 6.

[369] 1971, 'How Do You Sleep', on *Imagine*, track 8.

[370] Anthony DeCurtis, 'John Lennon: All in All' in *John Lennon Anthology Booklet*, 1998, p 30.

[371] Wiener, *Come Together*, p 278.

[372] Quoted in Du Noyer, *John Lennon*, p 41.

[373] Lennon, 'The Fat Budgie', in *The Penguin John Lennon*, p 87.

[374] Coleman, *Lennon*, p 603.

[375] 1972, 'New York City', on John and Yoko / Plastic Ono Band with Elephant's Memory plus Invisible Strings, *Some Time In New York City*, disc 1, track 5.

[376] Hamill, 'Long Night's Journey into Day', in Cott and Doudna (eds), *The Ballad of John and Yoko*, p 152.

[377] Anthony DeCurtis, 'John Lennon: All in All' in *John Lennon Anthology Booklet*, 1998, p 32.

[378] Anon, 'John Lennon in Demonstration', *The Times*, 12 August 1971.

[379] Hamill, 'Long Night's Journey into Day', in Cott and Doudna (eds), *The Ballad of John and Yoko*, p 153.

[380] Wiener, *Come Together*, p 155.

[381] Ron Skoler, 'An Interview with John & Yoko', *Rock*, 14 August 1972, quoted in Wiener, *Come Together*, p 210.

[382] John Lennon, quoted in Wiener, *Come Together*, p 209.

[383] 1972, 'The Luck Of The Irish', on, *Some Time In New York City*, disc 1, track 7.

[384] John Lennon, quoted in Wiener, *Come Together*, p 209.

[385] 1972, 'Sunday Bloody Sunday', on *Some Time In New York City*, disc 1, track 6.

[386] Lennon, *Skywriting by Word of Mouth*, p 144.

[387] Coleman, *Lennon*, p 660.

[388] Henke, *Lennon Legend*, p 49.

[389] 1972, 'New York City', on *Some Time In New York City*, disc 1, track 5.

390 Robertson, *The Art and Music of John Lennon*, p 156.

391 John Lennon, Review of *The Goon Show Scripts*, in *The New York Times*, 30 September 1973, quoted in Robertson, *The Art and Music of John Lennon*, p 163.

392 Du Noyer, *John Lennon*, p 72.

393 1973, 'I Know (I Know)', on John Lennon, *Mind Games*, track 10.

394 1973, 'Aisumasen (I'm Sorry)', on *Mind Games*, track 3.

395 Henke, *Lennon Legend*, p 55.

396 Sheff, *Last Interview*, p 206.

397 Du Noyer, *John Lennon*, p 81.

398 Sheff, *Last Interview*, p 206-207.

399 Chet Flippo, 'The Private Years', in Cott and Doudna (eds), *The Ballad of John and Yoko*, p 161.

400 Robertson, *The Art and Music of John Lennon*, p 163.

401 Du Noyer, *John Lennon*, p 81.

402 Baird, *John Lennon My Brother*, p 140.

403 Fawcett, *John Lennon*, p 135.

404 Ringo Starr interview sheet, annotated by John Lennon, included in Henke, *Lennon Legend*, p 54.

405 Du Noyer, *John Lennon*, p 91.

406 1974, 'Nobody Loves You When You're Down And Out', on John Lennon (with The Plastic Ono Nuclear Band), *Walls And Bridges*, track 11.

407 Hamill, 'Long Night's Journey into Day', in Cott and Doudna (eds), *The Ballad of John and Yoko*, p 150.

408 Robertson, *The Art and Music of John Lennon*, p 174.

409 Hamill, 'Long Night's Journey into Day', in Cott and Doudna (eds), *The Ballad of John and Yoko*, p 150.

410 Keith Badman, *The Beatles Years, Volume 2: After The Break-Up, 1970-2001* (Omnibus Press, London: 2001) p 149.

411 Robertson, *The Art and Music of John Lennon*, p 204.

412 Badman, *The Beatles Years, Volume 2*, p 154.

413 Hamill, 'Long Night's Journey into Day', in Cott and Doudna (eds), *The Ballad of John and Yoko*, pp 147, 155.

414 Coleman, *Lennon*, p 681.

415 F Scott Fitzgerald, *The Crack-Up*, quoted in Margaret Drabble (ed.), *The Oxford Companion to English Literature* (Oxford University Press, Oxford: 1985) p 352.

416 Robertson, *The Art and Music of John Lennon*, p 204.

417 Fawcett, *John Lennon*, p 187.

418 Badman, *The Beatles Years, Volume 2*, p 157.

419 John Lennon, *Real Love: The Drawings For Sean* (Little, Brown, London: 1999) p 18.

420 1971, 'Imagine', on *Imagine*, track 1.

421 Davies, *The Beatles*, p 57.

422 Sheff, *Last Interview*, p 6.

[423] Geoffrey Giuliano, *Lennon in America, 1971-1980* (Robson Books, London: 2001) p 122.

[424] Andy Peebles, *The Lennon Tapes*, p 76.

[425] Lennon, *Daddy, Come Home*, p 199.

[426] Lennon, *Daddy, Come Home*, pp 201-202.

[427] Mimi Smith, 'Aunt Mimi Answers To John On Tape', broadcast 6 January 1992 in Episode 207 of Westwood One's radio series, *The Lost Lennon Tapes*, quoted in Coleman, *Lennon*, pp 65-66.

[428] Wiener, *Come Together*, p 285.

[429] Elton John, card to John Lennon, October 1980, quoted in Bill Swainson (ed), *Encarta Book of Quotations* (Bloomsbury, London: 2000) p 557.

[430] John Lennon, postcard to Bob Gruen, March 1977, quoted in Coleman, *Lennon*, p 660.

[431] Badman, *The Beatles Years, Volume 2*, p 243.

[432] Giuliano, *Lennon in America*, p 122.

[433] 1978, 'The Great Wok', on John Lennon, *John Lennon Anthology*, disc 4 (Dakota), track 20.

[434] Du Noyer, *John Lennon*, p 116.

[435] John Lennon and Yoko Ono, 'Love Letter From John And Yoko To People Who Ask Us What, When And Why', in *The New York Times*, 27 May 1979, p 20E.

[436] Badman, *The Beatles Years, Volume 2*, p 235.

[437] F Scott Fitzgerald, *The Great Gatsby* (Penguin, Harmondsworth: 1990) p 177.

[438] Sheff, *Last Interview*, pp 77-78.

[439] Badman, *The Beatles Years, Volume 2*, p 259.

[440] 1980, 'Mr Hyde's Gone (Don't Be Afraid)', on John Lennon, *John Lennon Anthology*, disc 4 (Dakota), track 16.

[441] Badman, *The Beatles Years, Volume 2*, p 257.

[442] 1980, 'Beautiful Boy', on John Lennon and Yoko Ono, *Double Fantasy*, track 7.

[443] 1980, 'Woman', on John Lennon and Yoko Ono, *Double Fantasy*, track 10.

[444] 1980, 'Dear Yoko', on John Lennon and Yoko Ono, *Double Fantasy*, track 12.

[445] Jonathan Cott, 'The Last *Rolling Stone* Interview', in Cott and Doudna (eds), *The Ballad of John and Yoko*, p 192.

[446] John Chartres, 'Merseyside mourns working-class hero', in *The Times*, 10 December 1980 p 1.

[447] Hamill, 'Long Night's Journey into Day', in Cott and Doudna (eds), *The Ballad of John and Yoko*, p 154.

[448] Wenner, *Lennon Remembers*, p 188.

[449] 'John Lennon and Dorinish Island' at http://www.iol.ie/~beatlesireland/irish/irish1/dorinishisland.htm (30 July 2005).

[450] 1980, 'Dear John', on John Lennon, *John Lennon Anthology*, disc 4 (Dakota), track 19.

JOHN LENNON'S SONGS FOR THE BEATLES

Though it is not easy to separate Lennon from McCartney, an approximate list of John Lennon's likely contributions as a songwriter to the group's repertoire may be useful. Titles in italics are thought to be substantial collaborations, usually with Paul.

Released 1963:
Please Please Me; Do You Want To Know A Secret; There's A Place; It Won't Be Long; All I've Got To Do; Not A Second Time; This Boy.
Ask Me Why; I Saw Her Standing There; Misery; From Me To You; Thank You Girl; She Loves You; I'll Get You; Little Child; Hold Me Tight; I Want To Hold Your Hand; I Wanna Be Your Man.

Released 1964:
You Can't Do That; I Call Your Name; A Hard Day's Night; I Should Have Known Better; If I Fell; I'm Happy Just To Dance With You; Tell Me Why; Any Time At All; I'll Cry Instead; When I Get Home; I'll Be Back; I Feel Fine; No Reply; I'm A Loser; I Don't Want To Spoil The Party.
And I Love Her; Baby's In Black; Eight Days A Week.

Released 1965:
Ticket To Ride; Yes It Is; You've Got To Hide Your Love Away; You're Going To Lose That Girl; Help!; It's Only Love; Run For Your Life; Norwegian Wood (This Bird Has Flown); Day Tripper; Nowhere Man; Girl.
Wait; In My Life; We Can Work It Out; Michelle; What Goes On; The Word.
Released 1966:
Rain; I'm Only Sleeping; She Said, She Said; And Your Bird Can Sing; Tomorrow Never Knows; Dr Robert.

Released 1967:
Strawberry Fields Forever; Lucy In The Sky With Diamonds; Being For The Benefit Of Mr. Kite; Good Morning, Good Morning; All You Need Is Love; I Am The Walrus.
Penny Lane; With A Little Help From My Friends; Getting Better; She's Leaving Home; A Day In The Life.

Released 1968:
Revolution 1; Dear Prudence; Glass Onion; The Continuing Story Of Bungalow Bill; Happiness Is A Warm Gun; I'm So Tired; Julia; Yer Blues; Everybody's Got Something To Hide Except For Me And My Monkey; Sexy Sadie; Cry Baby Cry; Revolution 9; Goodnight.
Baby You're A Rich Man.

Released 1969:
Hey Bulldog; Don't Let Me Down; The Ballad Of John And Yoko; Come Together; I Want You (She's So Heavy); Because; Sun King; Mean Mr. Mustard; Polythene Pam.

Released 1970:
Across The Universe; You Know My Name (Look Up The Number); Dig A Pony; One After 909; Dig It.
I've Got A Feeling.
Released posthumously:
Real Love.
Free As A Bird.

SONG INDEX

GENERAL INDEX